Better Homes and Gardens®

step-by-step

ultimate

yard &

garden

Meredith® Books
Des Moines, Iowa

Meredith Books
1716 Locust Street
Des Moines, Iowa 50309–3023
www.meredithbooks.com

First Edition. Printed in United States.
ISBN: 978-0-696-23966-3 (Tradepaper edition)
978-0-696-23528-3 (Comb-bound edition)

Compiled from Better Homes and Gardens® *Perennial Gardens* and Better Homes and Gardens® *Garden Color*.

step-by-step ultimate yard & garden

introduction **6**

Before you jump eagerly into planning and designing your perennial gardens, take time to delight in a few ideas for creating the best arrangements. These pages provide a brief overview of some of the elements—color, plant habit, height—that make a successful garden beautiful and ever-changing.

the gardens **12**

You may find it difficult to pick only one kind of garden when you see all of the different styles that are readily achievable—from a border overflowing with color all season and plantings that attract birds and butterflies to designs for shady situations and Xeriscape climates.

the basics **82**

Planning a garden is only the beginning. You also need the fundamentals you will learn about in this section to help you have a successful and delightful experience in planting, maintaining, and accessorizing the beds and borders you design.

the plants **100**

Here are the best perennials for your garden, with details about use, color, fragrance, bloom time, and care. Sections on ferns, ornamental grasses, and irises offer additional selections to enhance your garden design.

color overview 132

Become a garden artist by looking at your yard as a potential kaleidoscope of color. See how you can conjure the magic of color to create a dazzling garden of ever-changing and lasting beauty.

colors & their companions 138

See how color affects you and your garden. Master the art of plant selection and explore time-tested plant combinations. Color your world restful, exciting, soothing, or whatever your heart desires.

schemes & themes 184

Discover how to choose an ideal blend of plants to create harmonious color palettes for your garden designs and outdoor decor. Paint with foliage, go tropical, brighten shade, color by number in pots, and more.

inspirational gardens 250

Add color to your yard and keep it going from season to season and year to year no matter where you live. Tour artists' gardens to gather ideas and inspiration for your personal space.

color decor 292

Use color, whether bold or subtle, as a personal expression of style. Decorate your outdoor settings, choosing furnishings and accessories for their year-round color and charm. Step-by-step projects make it easy.

sources 310

USDA hardiness map 312

introduction

perennial versatility

Before you begin selecting plants in your favorite colors, take a close look at your yard and discover the range of perennials you can use. Find out the amount and type of sun an intended garden receives; you'll find a range of lovely perennials for shade or light shade in addition to the beautiful ones for full sun. Consider how and when you spend your leisure time; you can find low-maintenance plants, flowers that glow in the evening, and plants that attract butterflies and birds. Think about your entire yard. Look for tall plants to set beside fences, short spreading plants to place along a path or in spaces between stepping-stones, and vining perennials to cover an arbor.

One of the best characteristics of perennials is that you don't need to replant them every year as you do annuals. You might dig and divide them every few years, but you can skip the yearly task that annuals require, giving you more time to enjoy the garden you've designed!

color

Colors are irresistible, even a lush cottage-style garden has a planned exuberance. To get the most out of the shorter bloom time of most perennials, select yours so plants bloom successively from spring through fall.

Remember some of the basics of color. Blues and violets are cool colors; they tend to recede in a garden. Reds, yellows, and oranges are hot; they "pop" in a border. Silver, white, and green—from pale to chartreuse to dark, and every hue in between—are neutral; they help harmonize groups of contrasting colors.

Combining colors well is a relatively easy art to master. Begin with shades of a main color—blue, violet, lavender, purple—add a few clumps of a contrasting yellow or red, and intersperse white flowers or silvery foliage.

color harmony
above: Tone down bright colors—yellow, orange, and red—with touches of white and silver to keep them from overwhelming your garden design.

texture
right: Combine plants that have different foliage and flower textures to add interest to the garden, as these feathery plumes of astilbe and narrow spikes of veronica do.

sunny splash

above left: Bold colors and sunny locations go together. Appropriate in any season, they are especially welcome in fall when skies seem bluer and trees are beginning to shed their multicolored leaves.

shady palette

left: Spring is the dominant season for gardens in shade. Flower colors may be fleeting, so depend on plants with boldly textured and variegated leaves, like these hostas, to light up the area through summer and fall.

color contrast

above: Blue, red, and yellow are contrasting colors. Their primary hues bring vibrant excitement to a garden. Use shades or tints of the primary colors—lavender and rose, for example—to create a subtle, equally attractive design.

sizing things up

Tall plants are magnificent. Because they usually spread somewhat in relation to their height, they can fill a garden quickly, making it look lush and mature much faster than if you planted mostly lower-growing perennials. You do, however, need to use them wisely, as a backdrop, an enclosure, or a screen for the entire garden bed.

Midheight perennials are the mainstay of a garden—partly because there are so many of them. Remember that medium-size plants grow between 2 and 4 feet. If you have a small garden or yard, you may want to use the taller of these perennials as your backdrop, rather than go for 5- to 6-foot plants, to keep the bed in scale with the rest of the yard.

Low-growing perennials can play many roles in the landscape. They are perfect for edging a bed or border and make wonderful container plantings. If the plants are spreading types (such as creeping phlox and thyme), you can use them as groundcovers, as decorative accents in a dry stone wall, or to soften the hard edges of a retaining wall as they spill over the top.

When you design a garden, don't be too rigid about heights. Place a couple of midheight perennials toward the front of the bed. Perhaps set a tall plant at the side. The garden will look much more natural and "uncomposed" if you intermingle plant heights a bit. Nature, of course, may do that for you. Plants that readily reseed themselves, such as columbine, corydalis, and knautia, are not particular about where their seeds drop and germinate, so you will always find surprises in the border the following spring. Take advantage of them.

tall specimens

right: Borrow a practice from the English and use perennials, such as crambe and ornamental grasses, not only in a border but also as specimen plants or in a mixed bed with shrubs. In a bed or border, set plants that grow 5 to 6 feet tall at the rear where they will form an imposing backdrop for midheight and shorter plants, such as beebalm and coreopsis.

ground covering

above: Plants that cover the ground quickly and thickly keep weeds from germinating, help prevent soil erosion on slopes, and create a carpet—a living mulch—in shady or sunny areas. If, like thyme, they also flower beautifully, they provide a delightful bonus.

habit forming

The way a plant grows influences how you will use it. Obvious? Not always. You can take advantage of the growth habit of some plants in not-so-obvious ways. Flowers with lax stems, such as knautia, will stand upright if you support them. Left to their own devices, they also will float or weave attractively among other, sturdier plants. Vines, such as the clematis below, usually climb, but they can also drape—effectively covering a retaining wall or spreading out as a groundcover among upright perennials.

Growth habit often enters into your design in your choices of tall, midheight, and short plants and of naturally bushy, vertical, and spiky plants. To create an interesting planting, combine groups of plants with different growth habits.

low spreading

above: Many low-growing plants, such as creeping phlox and dianthus, spread slowly enough that you can use them as edging plants in a border. Their foliage, often evergreen, stays attractive for months.

climbing high

left: A perennial vine like clematis can wind its way up a trellis, clamber over an arbor, camouflage a fence, or tumble across a stone wall. Flowers add to the beauty, but the shape, color, and texture of the foliage is most important for an all-season design.

introduction

looking closely

Gardening is more than planning and planting. The day-to-day joy is in the details, the closeup beauty, and, yes, the little miracles. Watching perennials appear above ground every spring, noticing the shape of a flower, burying your nose into a fragrant peony or lily, spotting a monarch sipping nectar from your carefully tended butterfly weed—these are the bonuses that only gardeners can enjoy on a regular basis. Be sure to take the time from your chores to get close to the natural world.

unusual plants

right: Look closely at your plants. Trilliums, for instance, with their tripartite configuration—three leaves, three sepals, and three petals—are worth a leisurely study. So are the tiny blooms that make up the flat-topped yarrow inflorescence (flower), the spurred flowers of columbine, and the beautiful falls and standards of an iris.

seasonal changes

below: In spring, fiddleheads emerge and gradually mature to the familiar lacy fronds we know as ferns. Some plants, such as balloon flowers, keep their presence unknown until much later—sometimes endangering their existence because we forget where we planted them the previous year.

statements

right: In addition to demanding attention with their color or fragrance, some plants show off with their particular form. Consider peonies, which have such noticeable yellow stamens, and purple coneflowers with their jaunty, dark, central disk. Such discoveries add to the pleasure of gardening.

planning the details

As you can see, there are probably as many aspects of gardening to notice as there are perennials to plant. Take into consideration the variety of shapes, colors, and fragrances that appeal to you, and think about how they might also entice and nurture wildlife. Think in terms of seasons: the clear greens of newly emerging foliage in spring, the forms of flowers in summer (low-growing, tall, single-flowered, or very double), and the changing hues of flowers and foliage in fall.

You can combine many different interests in one garden. To be successful, all you need to do in the beginning is think small and focus on a few different plants at a time. Don't go wild in your enthusiasm at first because you can—and undoubtedly will—enlarge a border and add plants as you learn more about them.

bird feasts

above: Seed-producing plants, such as purple coneflowers and ornamental grasses, entice birds to visit, and occasionally stay year-round in a garden.

fragrance

above: The ephemeral aspect of perennials is their fragrance. Many entice with their aromas: peonies, iris, lilies, dianthus, phlox, salvias, sweet woodruff. Even those that aren't technically fragrant, like ferns, have a fresh scent that makes you want to reach out and brush them as you pass by.

butterfly gems

left: The jewels of the air justify our planting for them simply by being there. Plants such as beebalm, gayfeather, and yarrow will bring butterflies to your yard.

the gardens

cottage gardens 14

entry gardens 18

beautiful borders 22

shade gardens 26

naturalistic gardens 30

butterfly gardens 36

multiseason interest 40

hillside gardens 44

xeriscape gardens 48

contemplative gardens 52

evening gardens 56

raised beds 60

edible treasures 64

garden paths 68

fences for gardens 78

cottage gardens

casual chic

Based on the heritage of English gardening, cottage-style designs might look casual and unplanned, but in reality, they take careful thought and a few years of growth to be truly beautiful. Basically, a cottage garden consists of a combination of perennials, shrubs (such as roses and camellias), and bulbs (for spring

a classic design

right and below: One of the joys of a cottage-style garden is the abundance of lush, changing colors over a long season. Foxgloves, hollyhocks, daisies, roses, and an arbor set the style in this garden.

perennials

1 ox-eye daisy, page 117

2 salvia, page 122

3 foxglove, page 113

4 yellow loosestrife, page 118

other plants

a 'joseph's coat' rose

classic arbor

above: **An arbor with seat provides a place for plants to climb and for you to sit to survey the results of your efforts.**

and summer color). Add ornamental grasses and a few perennial herbs, if you wish. You will undoubtedly want to put in some structures: an arbor, perhaps a fence as a backdrop, or a garden bench. While the garden is establishing itself, fill in vacant spaces with annual flowers.

in the beginning

The carefree beauty of your garden requires good site selection, soil preparation, and plants that are appropriate for your climate zone. The size of the garden depends on the size of your property and the amount of time you can devote to it. Carefree does not mean maintenance-free. Taking care of the garden gives you opportunities to enjoy it up close and personal.

ultimate yard & garden | **15**

time	skill
weekend	experienced

you will need

- protractor, T square, triangle
- five 2×4s (for rafters)
- saber saw and carpenter's level
- mending plates or corrugated fasteners
- scrap lumber and string (temporary supports)
- posthole digger
- gravel
- four 10'-long 4×4 posts (redwood, red cedar, or pressure-treated lumber)
- ten 1×2s (for crossbars), length as desired
- 1×8 (spacer)
- galvanized nails and screws
- hammer and screwdriver
- wood preservative (optional)

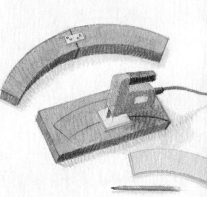

1

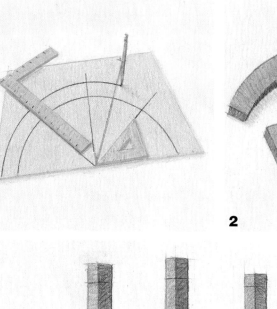

2

3

1 **plan** Use a protractor and T square to draw the curved section of the arbor on paper. The 8-foot tall arbor can be any width you want; 4 feet or wider is best.

2 **cut arch** Trace the pattern onto 2×4s. Cut out four sections for each side of the top using a sabersaw, and temporarily fasten the sections together using mending plates or corrugated fasteners.

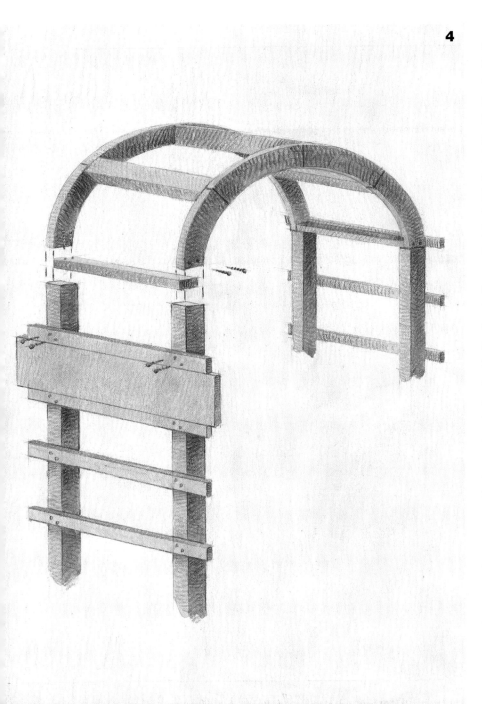

4

site posts Mark the exact location for the posts. Drive pegs in at all four corners, winding string tightly around them. Check that the sides are parallel and the front and back square to the sides. Remove the pegs and dig 2-foot holes with a posthole digger. Fill bottom of holes with 4 inches of gravel and insert the posts. Nail temporary supports between the posts to hold the posts in place while you pack soil into holes for stability. Remove the supports and stakes after nailing on the first crossbars. **3**

arch and spacing Nail one 2×4 to the top of each side. Screw the two joined arch pieces to the ends of the 2×4s, making sure that the mending posts are on the inside. Then nail a crossbar over each 2×4 to cover it. Nail the first crossbars 12 inches above the ground, using a level to ensure they are even and parallel to each other. After you attach the first crossbar, place a 1×8 on top of it, rest the next crossbar on it, and nail the crossbar in place with two nails for each side. Use the board as a guide to space the remaining side crossbars evenly. Screw three rafters between the two arches— one at each of the three arch "joints." (Notch the ends of the rafters to accommodate the mending plates.) **4**

Sand any rough edges. Treat exposed ends with a wood preservative.

entry gardens

zones	exposure
4–9	sun or light shade

planning your entryway

Front-yard gardens usually show off your best efforts. Here are a few guidelines that will help make the most of your planning and work.

Coordinate the style of your entry garden with that of the house. To ensure that its design adds to the beauty of the house rather than detracts from it, consider both as one entity. Almost any style of garden can enhance a Colonial, English, or French design. A wild or cottage look is inappropriate for a contemporary or a Victorian-style house. Similarly, a very formal garden would look wrong around a Cape Cod or Saltbox house.

Aim for an open view along the walkway from the street to the front door as well as across the

a warm welcome

right and below: **The North American way of planting a front-yard garden is turning away from the mundane foundation plantings of junipers, rhododendrons, and yews, which block windows in a matter of years or take hours of pruning to stay within bounds. Instead, the emphasis is on the unusual—the seasonal interest that colorful perennials provide. Delphiniums and foxgloves provide height and are airy enough to see through.**

perennials

1 delphinium, page 112

2 artemisia, page 107

3 dianthus, page 112

4 ox-eye daisy, page 117

5 cranesbill, page 114

other plants

a sweet alyssum

b climbing rose

c petunia

d geranium

front of the house. For a sense of privacy, intersperse tall plants among shorter, bushier ones, especially in front of windows. Tall and airy perennials, such as delphiniums, foxgloves, lilies, and bugbane, interrupt a view; they do not obstruct it.

Build an entry or foundation planting with year-round appearance in mind because it must be a garden for all seasons. Place a few evergreen shrubs strategically to provide structure and interest in seasons when the perennials are dormant. Set tall shrubs near corners; place low-growing ones among the perennials or as a backdrop for them.

Consider exposure and the amount of direct sun your entry receives. With a north or northeast exposure, you might need to augment perennials with annuals, small trees, and groundcovers because many shade-loving perennials bloom only in spring.

country look

right: A fairly narrow bed along the foundation in front of a long, low house adds seasonal color as well as year-round structure and interest. Foxgloves, delphiniums, bellflowers, and lilies mix with annual begonias, candytuft, cosmos, and zinnias. Backed by broad-leaved evergreens, the border is more interesting than the old-fashioned foundation plantings of shrubs you may be used to seeing. Window boxes filled with pansies, nasturtiums, and lobelia provide even more color for the summer months. The abundant plantings—reminiscent of a cutting garden—camouflage the dying foliage of spring-flowering bulbs, which begin the show in April with daffodils and grape hyacinths and continue it into May with tulips. Remember all the seasons of the year when you design a garden, whether the planting is in the front, side, or back. Include evergreen material so the bed has color and interest year round.

contrasting colors

left: Reds, yellows, and white brighten an entry corner. Lilies, black-eyed Susans, and penstemons provide summer color, and evergreen dwarf Alberta spruces and yews provide the planting structure through the winter months.

warm shades

below: Layers of color greet passersby and visitors at the entry garden of this English-style house. The warm hue of the fieldstone and the stark contrast of the white stucco form the backdrop for a kaleidoscope of multicolor roses, foxgloves, and calla lilies, contained in raised beds by a low wall of matching stone. The lush bed on the right, backed by a higher stone wall, hides a small patio from the view of the street.

beautiful borders

zones	exposure
4–9	sun or light shade

color

Consider how colors affect the overall feel of the garden. Blues and violets are receding, cool colors, making a garden seem larger. Bold reds, oranges, and yellows are warm colors; too much can overwhelm a small plot.

Group colors and plants and repeat them along the length of the border. Because of the differences in flower and leaf shapes and growth habits, the grouping of white iris, peonies, and columbines, *right,* for example, has a larger impact than an equal-size planting of only one of these species,

border basics

right: For beauty as well as ease of maintenance, plant your borders with perennials; use annuals to fill in empty spaces and provide edging with continuous bloom. To achieve a balanced design, plan the garden on paper first.

shape

Use a mix of plant shapes: mat (dianthus), cushion (euphorbia), mounded (sedum), narrow (fountain grass), strap-shape (iris), airy (baby's breath), and spiky (veronica).

Vary the shape and texture of foliage because few perennials bloom for an entire season. Choose foliage that is an attribute when the flowers are gone. Leaves may be coarse (bergenia) or fine (meadow rue), rounded (hosta) or lance-shape (coreopsis), glossy (black snakeroot) or velvety (lamb's-ears), variegated (heliopsis) or silver (artemisia).

perennials

1 peony, page 119

2 columbine, page 107

3 bearded iris, page 130

4 foxglove, page 113

5 dianthus, page 112

border know-how

For the most impressive planting, make your garden as deep as 6 feet. That may seem large, but it will provide enough space for bigger, varied plantings. A 6- to 9-foot depth is room to layer groups of plants—from lowest to tallest—rather than to string out several individual specimens.

The garden may look sparse when you first plant it, but within two to three years, the perennials will spread to cover the vacant spaces. Resist the impulse to set plants closer than the recommended mature spacing. Most perennials will grow 2 to 3 feet or more in circumference. If you crowd plants when they are young, they are less likely to be healthy (without the benefit of good air circulation around them), and you will need to dig them up and divide them before too long.

To access all of the areas of a deep border,

1 early summer For bounteous color all season, select perennials that bloom early, midseason, and late. At the beginning of summer, you might select black-eyed Susans, coreopsis, daylilies, blanket flowers, and lilies. Edge the border with low-growing annuals that will flower all season: marigolds, ageratum, petunias, and zinnias. You may want to choose a color scheme for each season and use that color as a backbone of the garden.

2 midsummer For midsummer, when temperatures are hottest and water may be scarce, add cooling colors. Clumps of white and pink phlox with blue and purple delphinium and veronica contribute eye-pleasing shades as well as vertical accents to the garden. Other good bloomers include balloon flower, scabiosa, lavender, cupid's dart, butterfly weed, globe thistle, bugbane, and beebalm.

3 fall Chrysanthemums are most important for continued color in the garden from late summer through fall. Blue-flowered asters and hardy ageratum, yellow-flowered goldenrod and helianthus, purple-flushed turtlehead, and rosy obedient plant contribute autumn blooms as well. Fall is the season when you may be most aware of foliage shape, texture, and color, from hostas and coralbells to artemisia and ornamental grasses.

place stepping-stones or pavers strategically for an integral, pleasing part of the design.

beyond plants

There is more to a good border design than plants. In addition to a few stepping stones, you might want to lay an informal path to bisect the border so you can walk right into the garden. Create another destination by setting an arbor or a bench at the end of the path.

Augment perennials with decorative containers of annuals and small shrubs. Invite birds into the border with a birdbath secluded among medium or tall plants.

Selectively—*very selectively*—place statues or other works of art into the garden. Edge the border, if you want, with a low barrier of wrought iron, terra-cotta, or wood. Or spade a trench to keep the perimeter neat and the border clear of the roots of invading grass and weeds.

shade gardens

zones	exposure
4–9	shade or light shade

planning

The kind of garden you can plant depends on the type of shade you have, the growth habit of the surrounding trees and shrubs, and the soil characteristics. Perennials must

subtle beauty

right and below:
Perennials for shade gardens are exquisite. Many bloom in spring before the trees leaf out and create a covering canopy. Quite a few, such as the astilbe and leopard plant (not yet blooming), flower in summer. Like the hosta and fern, their foliage is so attractive that the plants deserve a place in the garden even if they never flowered.

perennials

1 astilbe, page 108

2 leopard plant, page 117

3 fern, pages 126–127

4 hosta, page 116

other plants

a wintercreeper

compete with the trees for moisture, nutrients, and space, so it is easier to plant under deep-rooted trees, such as oaks, than under shallow-rooted maples. Damp shade supports more plants than dry shade. High canopies allow more sun to reach the plants than low-branching evergreens. Raise the canopy by pruning off the lowest limbs. Deciduous trees allow sun into the garden in early to midspring, which is an advantage for selecting plants, but observe how the light quality and intensity change before you plant.

selecting plants

Foliage texture and color are most important in a shade garden. Flowers are ephemeral; foliage brings substance and interest to the area for the longest season.

ultimate yard & garden | **27**

plants for shady gardens

Think of the various shades of green: chartreuse, bluish, grayish, pale, dark. Envision leaves edged with cream, white, yellow, or burgundy. Contemplate those with smooth, crinkled, and puckered textures; plants with simple or very bisected; rounded, heart–shape, or spiky; small or gigantic leaves.

Add flowers, however brief their season, and such a garden will bring lovely, cool, and soothing aspects to the yard.

plants that like shade

- astilbe
- hardy begonia
- bleeding heart
- columbine
- coralbells
- corydalis
- dead nettle
- ferns

- hellebore
- hosta
- jacob's ladder
- lungwort
- primrose
- sweet woodruff
- virginia bluebells
- wild ginger

shady colors

opposite: Sweet woodruff carpets the ground along a woodland walk beside a stream. The shade garden is filled with rhododendrons, azaleas, ferns, and iris.

far left: Cinnamon fern and white-flowered wood anemones grow in the shade of a silverbell tree.

left: Delicate yellow blooms of corydalis, a plant for sun or light shade, brighten a corner filled with hostas.

below: In moist soil in light shade, yellow flag blooms with ferns and hostas—all three do well in damp locations.

naturalistic gardens

zones	exposure
3–10	sun

worth a garden

Birds love natural gardens because they can find all they need to survive in them. Seed heads of perennials and ornamental grasses provide food. Shrubs, trees, and some perennials offer shelter and nesting places. A birdbath contains water for drinking and bathing. You, meanwhile, gain the benefit of natural pest control because many birds eat hundreds of insects daily.

When you plan a natural wildlife garden, include a diverse selection of plants—trees, shrubs, grasses, perennials, and annuals that reseed. Birds and other wildlife won't care if you have the latest cultivars; in fact, they prefer species and older varieties. Look for plants indigenous to your area, because they will look the most natural in it.

back to nature

right and below: **The wild, somewhat unkempt look of a naturalistic garden is misleading. The garden takes as much planning as a formal design does. It also requires preliminary work—weed removal, good soil preparation, and appropriate plant selection. The rewards are in the seasonal changes you can observe in the plants, such as these grasses and sedum, and the wildlife visitors you will see flying and creeping around.**

perennials

1 'autumn joy' sedum, page 123

2 russian sage, page 120

3 feather reed grass, page 128

4 pampas grass, page 128

maintenance

Be less than vigilant about grooming the garden and the plants. Let many of the flowers go to seed, especially late in the season, to provide birds a source of food. Pull out or transplant seedlings that germinate too prolifically or in places you don't want them. Wait until the following spring to cut back the plumes of ornamental grasses rather than cutting them in autumn.

Be careful about using any kind of pesticide in the garden. When you must use one, do so at night when birds will not be foraging for food.

You may not love all the wildlife your garden attracts. Raccoons and groundhogs can be a nuisance and might eat your vegetables and flowers. Deer are difficult to protect against. Be prepared to share some of your favorite flowers and vegetables with nature's creatures.

glorious grasses

above: Ornamental grasses—ruby-colored fountain grass, Japanese blood grass, and sedge—and salvias are easy-care plants that provide cover and food for birds and other small animals.

cooling effects

right: Hot, dry sites can be floriferous if you take advantage of the shade cast by deciduous trees and shrubs.

long-lived plants

left: Purple coneflower and coreopsis form a delightful complementary pair in any garden. The color contrast is particularly effective in the wildflower look of a naturalistic design.

bird friendly

below left: A lush garden with salvias *(Salvia coccinea* and *S. leucantha),* 'Powis Castle' artemisia, and tall, purple-spired fountain grass surrounds a dovecote. Species of salvia are especially attractive to hummingbirds, as are the jasmine flowers covering the tuteur on the left. You may see wrens, chickadees, and titmice balancing on the waving stems of the grass.

sunny color

below: For a sunny border, black-eyed Susans, sedum, purple coneflower, and blue-flowered Russian sage make neat clumps of color. These plants are not invasive. All of them have a long bloom season, and their flowers or seed heads last well into winter, providing a natural source of food for birds that do not fly away to warmer climates.

time	skill
1–2 hours	easy

you will need

hoe or shovel

protective gear: rubber gloves, safety glasses, dust mask

spray bottle and water

3 gallons premixed concrete

peat moss

crushed, colored, recycled glass

rock specimens

sheet of plastic

for songbirds

This special handmade birdbath belongs nestled in a flower bed where admirers will never know that it was so easy to make. You don't need a fancy mold to fashion the 18- to 20-inch basin. You can even use a cardboard box instead of the ground, as long as the box is at least 4 inches wider than the basin's width. Fill it 10 inches deep with soil; then scoop a basin shape in the soil.

1 mold Dig and shape a hole in the ground (or in a cardboard box filled with 10 inches of soil) as a mold. Sprinkle the shape with water and pack down the soil firmly. Tamp a flat area in the center so the finished basin will sit securely on a flat surface.

2 mix Wear protective gear. Combine 3 gallons of premixed concrete with 2 to 3 cups of peat moss in a wheelbarrow. Add about 2 gallons of water and quickly mix with a hoe to make a stiff batter. If it is too thin, add more concrete; if too thick to hold together, add water.

3 form Work quickly, concrete starts to set in minutes. Shovel the wet mix into the mold. Scoop concrete from the center of the basin to the outside rim. Pat it into place, conforming it to the shape of the basin. Pat smooth. Spritz with water to keep concrete moist.

4 finish Decorate the basin by sprinkling crushed, recycled glass on the wet mix; press gently into place. You also can use other decorative pieces such as stones. Cover the basin with a plastic sheet; let cure for 3 to 7 days. Uncover; let age for 1 month before filling with water.

butterfly gardens

zones	exposure
4–10	sun

warmth and water

Butterflies need the warmth of the sun and appreciate a flat stone or two for basking. You will see them gather in groups if you provide a shallow puddle where they can drink. Protect them from strong

winged jewels

right and below: Butterflies are a delight to watch as they float around the garden on a breeze, alighting briefly on nodding flowers. Attract them by planting a few perennials and shrubs for their larval needs and more for their nectar preferences, such as the beard-tongue, catmint, crambe, and veronica in this garden.

perennials

1 iris, pages 130–131

2 catmint, page 119

3 oriental poppy, page 120

4 speedwell, page 125

5 beard-tongue, page 120

6 foxglove, page 113

7 bellflower, page 110

8 crambe, page 111

winds with a garden near a few shrubs or trees that act as a windbreak.

plan the beauty

You can incorporate butterfly plants into an existing bed or border, such as that at left, or plant a separate garden. To a butterfly, fragrance is not as important as color, although it does play a role. The eyes of a butterfly perceive shades of yellow, red, and blue to lavender.

The best flowering plants for a butterfly garden are wild or species forms rather than hybrids, single-flowered instead of double-flowered, and tubular or flat-topped.

Plant in large groups; individual spots of color are less attractive than a broad wash of hues. Groups of 10 or more of the same color work well.

two winners

right: Beebalm and purple coneflower are two of the best plants for attracting butterflies. Plant groups of them around a weathered fountain, and shelter the garden with a backdrop of evergreens.

nectar and food plants

below: In July, large groups of colorful purple coneflower, phlox, gayfeather, beebalm, Shasta daisy, and black-eyed Susan mingle in a wild garden. Less colorful but almost as important are larval plants. Some butterflies are quite plant-specific, laying eggs on one type of plant. Monarchs, for example, lay their eggs only on milkweed. Others are more opportunistic, using a range of plants, from herbs such as dill and parsley, to trees such as cherry and tulip poplar. Include trees elsewhere in the yard if you do not want to incorporate them in the garden bed.

plants that attract butterflies

- anise hyssop
- beebalm
- black-eyed susan
- butterfly weed
- coreopsis
- dianthus
- garden phlox
- purple coneflower
- queen anne's lace
- red valerian
- thyme
- vervain

juicy fruit

above: Butterflies like sweet fruit. Put a slice of ripe papaya, orange, or banana near the edge of the garden and you can watch them feed.

nectar blooms

far left: Butterfly weed is a favorite nectar plant. Although there are new cultivars in various colors, stick to the species to attract butterflies to the garden.

rest stop

left: The jury is still out on the usefulness of butterfly houses. If the house doesn't lure them, the arching butterfly bush will.

multiseason interest

zones	exposure
3–9	sun or light shade

season to season

The beauty of a garden is not confined to one, two, or even three seasons. Whether you are out in its midst or gazing at it through a window, you want to see something attractive in the garden all year. With a bit of planning, you can.

looking ahead

right and below: **The beauty of a winter garden depends on the details: foliage and stem color, ever-present structure—from seed heads on perennials, and evergreen branches on conifers to accessories, such as benches—and play of light and shadow as the sun moves lower in the sky.**

perennials

1 sedge, page 128

2 zebra grass, page 129

3 sedum, page 123

4 black-eyed susan, page 122

other plants

a spruce

b pine

Color during the growing season, spring to fall, relies not only on flowers but also on foliage. Think of the dusky maroon leaves of some coralbells and 'Vera Jameson' sedum, the variegations of hostas and euonymus, the silver-gray of artemisia and lamb's ears, the red of Japanese blood grass, and the blue of blue oat grass. For winter, plant red- or yellow-stemmed dogwoods and berried shrubs or trees (roses, hollies, crabapples). The bright reds will seem to shimmer when backlit by the setting sun.

Pattern refers to leaf shapes as well as branch and growth habits. Although the leaves may be most noticeable in summer, the plant's habit takes on importance in winter when a dusting of snow accentuates it. Perennials left in the garden for winter, such as grasses, sedums, coneflowers, look wonderful topped with snow. Leafless branches of deciduous trees show the intricate designs you miss during the summer months; their shadows on lawns and snow are an integral part of the special quality a garden takes on in winter.

Structure includes the permanent parts of your garden: fences, arbors, trellises, rock outcroppings, and evergreen plantings. In many zones, perennials such as sea thrift, bergenia, and coralbells are evergreen, but for assured year-round interest, add shrubs such as boxwood, and ornamental grasses, such as fountain grass and maiden grass, to give the garden form.

winter

right: A good reason to be a little lazy when it comes to cleaning up the garden in fall is the presence that leftover plants lend to the landscape. Witness the fountain grass and sedum here, with snow capping their dried and drooping flower heads, and the coneflowers with their dark seed heads. Permanent elements, such as the brick path, provide a link to the garden design.

early summer

below: Start calling attention to this garden in early summer. These late-blooming plants don't get much notice in spring. That is the time to cut down the old sedum bloom stalks and the ornamental grasses. You could interplant spring-flowering bulbs, which would add early-season color among the perennials.

summer

left: At the height of the gardening season, color and shape abound. Delightful purple coneflower and bright black-eyed Susan contrast with the warm, celery-green flowers of 'Autumn Joy' sedum and the blue spires of Russian sage. Ornamental grasses (such as fountain grass) and daylilies provide vertical accents with their strap-shape leaves. The texture of the plumes on grasses adds to the garden design.

autumn

left: The fall season brings subtle color to the garden, interspersed with warm shades of oranges, yellows, and reds from sedums and chrysanthemums. This is the season for purple-blue asters and the tans and beiges of the fluffy plumes of ornamental grasses. Even as you cut back other perennials that have stopped blooming, enjoy the interplay of garden colors with those of the changing fall leaves on deciduous trees. Evergreen—or ever-colored—plants, such as purple-leaved coralbells, reveal their benefits in a multiseason garden.

hillside gardens

zones	exposure
3–10	sun

thwart erosion

Aside from the difficulty of trying to mow a hill or slope, you have the problems of drainage (too much, too fast) and soil erosion. Many plants, including perennials, help stabilize the soil. Grasses are among them, but turfgrass requires much work to maintain. Ornamental grasses, on the other hand, are often drought-tolerant, and need to be cut back once a year in spring. No lawn mower needed.

Good grasses for hillsides include many you would not want to put into a border because they can

rolling on

right: **A hillside— whether rocky, screelike, steep, or gentle—might not be an ideal place for a lawn. Turn it into a lovely garden like this with a variety of flowering groundcovers with texture and foliage that provide interest after the flowers have faded.**

become invasive. On a slope, their rampant growth and spread is fine. Sweet flag, switch grass, buffalograss, and ribbon grass are a few. Add some clumping grasses, such as fountain grass, oat grass, and little bluestem, and a few heaths, heathers, and creeping junipers for an attractive solution to a potential problem.

special gardens

Large rocks embedded in a gentle slope form microclimates that can create the perfect spot for special plants (such as alpines, cacti, and succulents) that might not survive in your climate under regular garden conditions.

plants

1 dianthus, page 112

2 sedum, page 123

3 speedwell, page 125

4 cranesbill, page 114

5 stone cress, page 106

6 snow-in-summer, page 110

7 aubretia, page 108

gentle slope

above left: An informal layering of bluestone holds in the soil at the bottom of this gentle slope and provides the perfect ledge for candytuft to spill over. Colorful yellow coreopsis, blue catmint, and silvery artemisia offer a long season of contrasts.

narrow access

above right: You can dress up even the narrowest bed, such as this one between two sets of stairs leading to a pair of Berkeley, California townhouses, with a variety of hardy succulents, including flowering jade, aloe, and crassulas.

steep ascent

right: Retaining walls made with the same stone as the stairs offer pockets for planting on this steep hillside. Low-growing, ground-covering shrubs guarantee that the beds will look good in all seasons, not only in summer. Bright spots of color—from annuals such as begonias and petunias to perennial groundcovers—turn the hillside into a lush, vibrant landscape.

stair softening

left: Very steep hillsides usually require a series of steps to make access easier. You can soften the stark look of stone, wood, or cement stairs if you leave a trough at the back of each tread and place creeping plants, such as thyme, baby's tears, and sedums, into it to spread over part of the steps. Set hostas, low-growing grasses, sedges, or ferns along the stairway to drape over the steps. Do not let the plants cover so much of the surface, however, that they threaten users' safety.

sedum subtleties

below: Sedums and sempervivums are excellent plants for rocky hillsides. Their various shades of green harmonize with early-blooming perennials, such as pink-flowered stone cress and cranesbill. Sedums are not invasive, and they are tolerant of drought and less-than-ideal soils and growing conditions—all three situations that they are likely to contend with on hilly locations.

xeriscape gardens

zones	exposure
5–11	sun or light shade

characteristics

Xeriscaping, using plants that have little or no need for water other than what rains provide, is adaptable to any section of the country. Focus on native wildflowers, trees,

look—no water

right and below:
Gardening without water or with water restrictions does not mean gardening without the beauty of flowers and the tantalizing effects of texture and form. You don't have to limit yourself to cacti and succulents (hardy or not), as beautiful as they are in this textural garden.

perennials

1 myrtle spurge, page 114

2 aeonium, page 106

3 prickly pear, page 119

4 hedgehog cactus, page 120

other plants

a buckwheat

b calylophis

and shrubs that have acclimated themselves to local growing conditions over the centuries. You might find that the allure of cacti is irresistible, especially after you have seen their bright, shimmering spring blooms next to crocus, grape hyacinth, and iris.

under the surface

Soil preparation, which is important for any garden, is paramount for a Xeriscape. The seemingly contradictory ability of the soil to retain water and also drain well is one of the secrets of dryscape gardening success. Plants that can withstand drought (cacti and succulents), many wildflowers (such as black-eyed Susan), and most ornamental grasses do not survive in standing water. Build up layers of gravel and grit before spreading a mix of sand, gravel, and soil on top, especially if you want to grow hardy cacti. Form the soil into mounds 4 to 5 inches high for the plants to grow on. Mulch with a ½-inch layer of stones and gravel.

garden oases

right: Take advantage of the microclimates you can create within a larger landscape. Here, dwarf conifers, alpines, and green and variegated iris survive heat and drought in summer; chives, prickly pears, and ornamental grasses take on winter cold—in a bed filled with amended soil to improve drainage and topped with stones to reflect light and absorb warmth. Group plants with similar needs (for example, a lot of direct sun or not much moisture) to make your maintenance chores easier.

hardy cacti

above: Opuntia, also known as rabbit ear, cholla, and prickly pear, is one of many cacti that will grow in cool climates. This pink form of *Opuntia basilaris* var. *aurea* is in a Detroit garden. Other cacti worth trying are the rather small columnar *Echinocereus* spp., with their large blooms, the pincushion cacti, *Coryphantha* spp., and other opuntia, from miniatures and shrublike bushes to *Opuntia compressa*—one of the hardiest.

warm-season color

left: Use touches of contrast to brighten a basically one-color garden. Here, a cutleaf Japanese maple anchors the corner of a bed filled with iris, feather grass, and lilyturf. Plant forms offer another opportunity for contrast—the grasslike foliage of lilyturf and the strap-shape leaves of the iris.

ultimate yard *&garden* | **51**

contemplative gardens

zones	exposure
3–11	light shade

the elements

To design a garden that is a cool and inviting retreat, consider including a gravel path; water in the form of a simple fountain, pond, stream, or birdbath; stone statuary; moss for soft texture and attractive color; evergreen and spring-flowering trees and shrubs; and perennials that will provide foliage interest after flowering.

Use plants that will give the effect of bamboo. Heavenly bamboo (*Nandina domestica*), which isn't a bamboo but a relative of barberry, has the bonus of red berries in fall and winter.

peaceful spots

right: **Contemplative gardens contain subtle colors. With a long heritage of Oriental horticultural practices, these gardens might be variations on shades of green, with few if any flowers. A small water feature, such as this bamboo fountain, is often included.**

Ornamental grasses, such as fountain and maiden grass, and reeds catch a breeze like bamboo does.

about bamboo

If you use bamboo, select clump-forming species instead of running bamboos, which require a fortresslike barrier (a 2- to 3-foot deep concrete edging) to prevent their taking over the yard. Clump-forming bamboos spread, but not as quickly or invasively. Among the most winter hardy are purple-tinted fountain bamboo (*Sinarundinaria nitida*, hardy to Zone 5) and yellow-green umbrella bamboo (*Thamnocalamus spathaceus*, hardy to Zone 6).

perennials

1 lilyturf, page 118

2 bamboo, page 129

3 bowles golden sedge, page 128

other plants

a japanese maple

ultimate yard & garden | **53**

shady retreats

right: Because it is difficult to be at ease for very long in the glaring sun, site your contemplative retreat in the shade. You can create a shady spot with plantings of bamboo or evergreen trees and shrubs or by enclosing the spot with a tall fence. (Bamboo makes a natural fence in one year of growth.) Add one or two spring-flowering trees, such as dogwood or redbud, and a deciduous tree, such as Japanese cutleaf or red maple, for brilliant fall color.

Foliage shapes, textures, and colors and plant forms are important. Bleeding heart, angel's trumpet, ferns, gunnera, hostas, iris, jack-in-the-pulpit, Japanese anemone, trillium, Solomon's seal, and Hakone grass will bring a variety of growth habits and flower colors to your garden from spring to late summer.

Make paths with wood rounds, small-size gravel or grit, or fine mulch so the paths will blend naturally with the surrounding garden.

quiet seating

above left: A bench sheltered among trees and leafy perennials is de rigueur. It provides a destination as well as a place to sit and think.

pleasant access

above right: A simple or a zigzag bridge—over a dry creek or a flowing stream—directs your passage and offers varying garden views.

artful visions

left: You'll usually find water in these gardens, whether in the form of a pond, a fountain, or a gentle waterfall. The sound of water masks street noises; the surface of still water creates a canvas onto which plant reflections are painted.

evening gardens

garden for your time

You undoubtedly know about the four-o-clock, which opens its pink, red, or yellow buds in late afternoon, and the annual moonflower (relative of the day-blooming morning glory). There are, however, many

enjoy the garden

right and below: It's all very well to design beautiful gardens, but if they are lovely to look at only during daylight hours, they won't satisfy you if you're not home to see them. That's where evening gardens come to the rescue. They contain plants that blossom in the evening or have light-colored flowers that shine through in the darkness.

perennials

1 white bleeding heart, page 112

2 hellebore (lenten rose), page 115

3 hellebore (christmas rose), page 115

4 wake-robin, page 125

5 european ginger, page 108

perennials whose scent is stronger or color more vibrant than in daylight hours that belong in an evening garden. Some flowers are showier in the subdued light of dusk.

coloring it up

Plants with silver or gray foliage (lamb's ears, dusty miller, artemisia, some coralbells varieties) belong in the garden. White flowers (lily, Shasta daisy, garden phlox, gooseneck loosestrife, yarrow, flowering tobacco, and feverfew) provide the classic color of an evening garden. Accents of pink (evening primrose and foxglove), blue (gayfeather and salvia), and yellow (daylily and 'Moonbeam' coreopsis) stand out in relief against the subtle monochromatic palette of silver and white. White-flowered annuals, such as sweet alyssum, geranium, petunia, snapdragon, and zinnia, contribute brightness to an evening garden.

seasonal scenes from a garden—early spring

right: A garden next to a porch offers comfortable opportunities for enjoying an evening garden. Select flowers that remain open at dusk: delphiniums in shades of white and pale blue; columbines in white, blue and white, and rose; astilbes with deep rose, pink, red, and white spires of blooms; and daylilies (there are varieties that stay open in the evening, in spite of their name).

midspring color

below: White is the color of choice for many evening gardens because its various shades bring the area to life—and sight—as the sun sets. White is also one of the most common colors in nature, whether it is in western bleeding heart, foamflower, candytuft, or roses such as 'Iceberg', 'Alba' and 'Ice' Meidiland, and 'Madame Hardy'. Scatter other colors among the whites; they will pop out against the neutral background. And always remember foliage—the different shapes and textures add dimension to the garden.

late-spring fragrance

above: Peonies are wonderful in any garden because of their large, gorgeous, fragrant blooms and their foliage, which sets off other plants throughout the season. Pale rose foxgloves will seem to glow in the evening next to creamy white columbines. Include other flowers with fragrance, such as dianthus, clematis, annual stock, four-o-clock, and vining moonflower, with its huge blooms. Scents tend to be much stronger in the evening.

raised beds

zones	exposure
4–9	sun or light shade

alternatives

Instead of coping with the inevitable erosion on uneven ground, such as that on a slope or rocky hillside, you can terrace the land with stone walls to create aesthetically pleasing raised beds that make attractive gardens near sunken patios and along paths.

preplanning

If you build a raised bed or wall yourself, lay stones without mortar (dry stone construction) and

above ground

right: Of the many reasons for creating a garden above the ground, one of the most critical is waterlogged soil; few plants survive well in constantly boggy soil. Another is the soil itself. In this clay hillside, it was more practical to build a raised bed and bring in good loam than to amend the poor soil.

limit the height of the wall to 3 feet. It can, of course, be shorter, as low as 12 inches high.

Use mostly flat stones; they make the construction rather like laying bricks. The weight of each course or layer of stones will help hold the stones in place. Tilting back the stones slightly also will help because the soil filled in the bed will secure them.

If you plan to plant in the crevices, fill the spaces with soil as you build. Set the plants in the soil when you have finished the wall.

plants

1 blue oat grass, page 129

2 thyme, page 124

3 sedum, page 123

zones	time	skill
4–8	2–4 days	moderate

you will need

- garden hose or rope
- spray paint
- shovel
- stakes
- carpenter's level
- string
- flat rocks, various sizes

filling it up

When the wall is finished, fill the bed with fertile soil enriched with organic matter such as compost. Water well and let the soil settle for a few days to a week before planting.

outdoor dressing

right: Although you can surround a raised bed with a number of different materials, from timber to bricks, a stone wall sets it off naturally. Building a dry stone wall is easier than constructing one with bricks and mortar, and your efforts will last longer than if you used wood.

1 shape Outline the edge of the bed using a rope or a garden hose. When you are pleased with the shape of the design, spray-paint the outline on the ground, so you will have a reference of the space you need to clear for the planting bed.

2 level Set the level of the stone wall by hammering stakes into the ground along the painted line, marking the height of the wall on each stake. Connect the marks with a taut string. Check again to make sure that the top of the wall is level all along its length.

3 stack Remove the grass inside the stakes. Tilt the stones down slightly and back into the bed for stability. To build the wall without mortar, fill the crevices between and behind the stones with soil. Use the string as a guide for height.

4 finish On a sloping site, adjust the string height to compensate for the slope so the finished wall appears level. Finish the top of the wall with large flat stones. If you want plants to grow in the wall, leave crannies for planting as you build.

edible treasures

zones	exposure
4–11	sun

perennial edibles

Asparagus and rhubarb are valuable additions to any garden because of their foliage. Asparagus has feathery leaves on stalks that grow 3 to 5 feet tall; use it in the background of a border, as long as you can access the plants to

mix and match

right and below: **There aren't many perennial vegetables—asparagus and rhubarb are two of the best known—but you can fill out a garden with a mix of other perennial edible herbs and flowers, as in this garden.**

perennials

1 thyme, page 124

2 dianthus, page 112

3 chamomile, page 110

4 lemon thyme, page 124

5 allium (chives), page 106

other plants

a nasturtium

b 'lemon gem' marigold

c calendula

harvest the spears. The large leaves of rhubarb make an architectural statement in any garden; use it as a specimen plant or as a focal point in a bed.

tasty selections

Perennial herbs include the tiny-leaved thymes (common, silver, and lemon) and the grayish-green and multicolored sages. Lemon balm, mints (peppermint, spearmint, orange mint, plain, and variegated), oregano, marjoram, rosemary, and lavender bring fragrance and texture to gardens. Plant them in a separate bed or mix them with your other perennial plants.

edible flowers

When you grow flowers to eat or to use as a garnish, never treat them with chemical sprays. Edible flowers include daylilies, scarlet runner beans, pansies, dianthus, calendulas, violets, and tulips, as well as herb flowers and, of course, roses.

scentsational

above: A mass of lavender comes into bloom as the flowers of chives begin to go past their prime. Think of season of bloom when you plan a fragrant or edible garden to have color in succession, just as you do in a border of perennial flowers. For year-round appeal, place an accent piece, such as a birdbath or sundial, centered or slightly off-center in the bed.

kitty comfort

right: Catnip will keep feline friends in ecstasy. A bonus for the gardener is the lovely gray-green shade of the foliage, which can be particularly effective with a background planting of common mint, with its deeper green leaves. Catnip, or catmint, is not as invasive as true mint—one reason being that cats keep it in check; protect it from foragers with a chicken wire enclosure until it becomes well established.

fragrant paths

left: A combination of raised and mulched beds with brick and gravel paths leads visitors to the front door. Texture and form are the emphasis here, although fleeting colors from late-spring and early-summer flowers add temporary interest. Clumps of lavender and oregano contrast with grasslike chives and Egyptian onions as well as with shrublike sage. Add silver and gray accents with the deeply divided leaves of globe artichoke, cardoon, or artemisia or the velvety foliage of lamb's ears.

In a raised-bed garden such as this, you could safely plant mint without fear of it taking over. In the ground, however, you should curtail its invasive tendency to spread by underground runners by planting it in a bottomless pot with the rim just above the soil level.

If you provide sage with ideal growing conditions, it, too, can threaten to take over a garden, but it is easy to restrain by pulling up young plants in spring.

garden paths: brick

zones	time	skill	exposure
3–11	weekend	moderate	sun to light shade

you will need

- shovel
- hose or rope
- porous weed mat (optional)
- pea gravel and builder's sand
- edging (optional)
- bricks
- tamper
- broom

a statement of style

A path can be made from a broad range of materials, but to some extent, your choice will depend on the impression you want to make. In informal and woodland gardens, for example, you may want gravel or mulchlike shredded

perennials

1 corydalis, page 111
2 foxglove, page 113
3 feverfew, page 124
4 ox-eye daisy, page 117
5 iris, pages 130–131

other plants

a rosa glauca

bark chips. Formal beds look best with grass paths or those of stone or brick set in mortar.

Setting the material (bricks, stepping-stones, or pavers) in sand instead of concrete or mortar results in an informal look. Such paths are easier and less expensive to lay, and they leave crevices for creeping plants.

A path does not have to be continuous. You can make an attractive path that stops at a focal point and begins again across a lawn or garden bed.

walking about

left: A brick path such as this—or any path in the yard— should not be a last-minute addition. It is more important than a means of getting from one place to another. A well-designed path adds to the overall impact of a garden, so plan carefully for it.

ultimate yard *& garden* | **69**

garden paths: brick

1 **design** With the exception of grass, brick paths are the most classic walkways in a garden. You can lay bricks in an amazing array of patterns and shapes, and the laying is relatively easy.

Use a garden hose or rope to lay out the path, making it at least 2 to 3 feet wide. To keep the width accurate, you may want to mark it with paint as you go. If you follow the slope of a slight incline, use a curve or series of loose curves to help reduce the grade; broaden the path sightly where it curves.

2 **dig** Remove the sod and dig the base of the walk for its entire length. The depth should equal the thickness of the brick plus 4 inches for a sand base and 2 inches for gravel. Check the depth as you dig to maintain an even base.

3 **underlay** When you have cleared the path, lay down porous weed mat, if you want, to help keep the path weed-free and to allow rain water to seep through. Shovel in about 2 inches of pea gravel and spread it evenly. Add 4 inches of builder's sand as a base for the bricks. To maintain the original edges of the path, hammer in garden or landscape edging, bending it where necessary to follow the curves of the design.

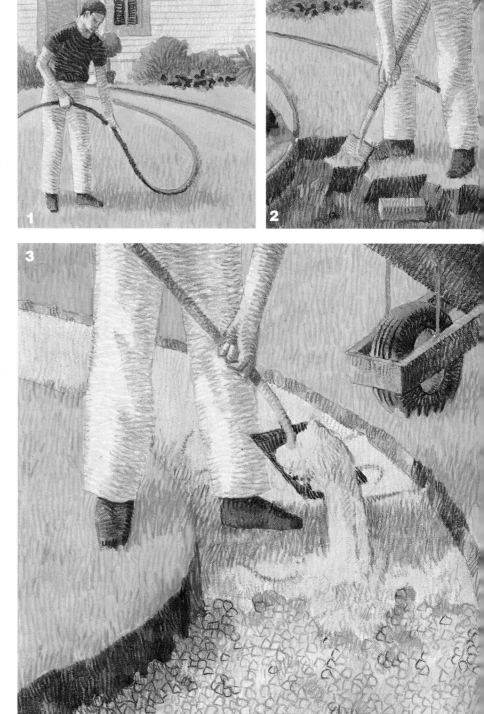

tamp Bricks need a firm, even surface **4** so if you place them, they will lay securely. Tamp the entire sand surface of the path. Use a level to check for accuracy.

lay bricks A number of patterns are **5** suitable for brick paths. Running bond, shown here, alternates the ends of the bricks. Stack bond lays each row of bricks evenly and end to end. Herringbone, basket weave, diagonal herringbone, and double basket weave are other attractive patterns. They require more time and skill to lay.

If you use old bricks, chip off excess mortar before placing them. Lay the bricks close together, moving in sections along the walk.

settle Pour sand over the bricks and **6** brush it into the crevices between. Brush away the excess. Let the path settle for a few days. You can hose the path with water to help settle the sand in the spaces. Add more sand if necessary. In areas with below-freezing winter weather, the alternate freezing and thawing of the ground beneath might heave some bricks out of place. You might need to reset some of the bricks each year.

During the growing season, pull weed seedlings that appear in the path.

garden paths: gravel

zones	time	level	exposure
3–11	weekend	easy	sun to light shade

undercover doings

When you dig out the walk, remove any tree and weed roots and rocks. You might want to lay a 1-inch-deep foundation of sand before you put down a weed mat, but it is not required.

For dry footing, lay a porous weed mat on top of the excavated walk. Do not use a nonporous black-plastic liner because it doesn't allow water to drain away.

Occasionally during the year, perhaps once every season, rake the gravel to smooth it. Blow fallen leaves or debris off the walk in autumn with the low setting on a yard/leaf blower.

simple gravel

right: **The most natural-looking path is one created with gravel, pebbles, stones, pine needles, or shredded bark. Gravel and small pebbles are the easiest to walk on. Pine needles can be slippery, especially when they are wet. Shredded bark and stones are often uncomfortable underfoot.**

perennials

1 thyme, page 124

2 saxifrage, page 123

3 allium, page 106

4 bellflower, page 110

5 sea pink, white, page 107

6 cranesbill, page 114

1 prepare Dig out the walk: 6 to 8 inches deep and 16 to 36 inches wide. A wider width will allow two people to walk abreast. If you want plants to spill over onto the gravel, make the walk wide enough to accommodate them without impeding foot traffic.

2 edge Place large stones or pavers along both sides of the walk to act as a retaining wall that will separate the gravel from the soil in the planting beds. For the most natural look, use stones that are indigenous to your area.

3 underlay Lay out the weed mat in the walk and cut it to the full width of the path plus 2 to 4 inches, following the curves and contours. Smooth and ease the mat around curves, a few wrinkles will not matter. Tuck the edges of the mat under the large stones.

4 fill Use a bucket to fill the walkway area with gravel. Smooth and level the surface rock with the back side of the rake. Backfill behind the large stones with the soil removed to make the walk, covering any of the mat that shows beyond the large stones.

ultimate yard & garden | **73**

garden paths: stepping-stones

zones	time	skill
3–11	weekend	moderate

you will need

- 12-inch plastic dishpan or storage container
- rubber gloves
- builder's sand
- trowel
- masonry mix
- large plastic bucket
- objects as desired, such as shells, rocks, leaves, pieces of broken pottery, or tiles

making the mix

Plan to use about one gallon of ready-mix masonry for each 12-inch stone. In a large bucket, make a well in the center of the dry mixture; pour in about one quart of water. Blend until the mixture is the consistency of custard; add more water if needed. Wear rubber gloves while you mix the masonry. Use the mixture immediately.

footwork

right: Crossing a lawn or traversing a garden bed, avoid leaving tracks in the grass or compacting the soil by marking the way with stepping-stones. Plain, unadorned stones are fine, but stones decorated with leaf impressions, shells, or other objects are particularly pretty. Use objects you have collected on vacations, flea market finds, leftover tiles, fern fronds, or large leaves.

perennials

1 thyme, page 124

2 speedwell, page 125

3 sedum, page 123

4 daylily, page 115

5 bellflower, page 110

6 gooseneck loosestrife, page 118

7 garden phlox, page 120

1 mold Fill a plastic container with damp sand to within 2 inches of the top. Trowel the top level. Press leaves into place, vein side up. Or embed a mix of shells or objects in the sand; the side placed in the sand will be visible when the mixture dries.

2 mix Pour moistened masonry mix carefully into the mold without disturbing the objects. Trowel to settle the mixture, release air bubbles, and bring excess water to the surface. Do not dig into the sand or overtrowel. The surface should be level and smooth.

3 cure Cure the mold in the shade for 48 hours. Loosen the mold and invert onto plastic. Trowel off the excess sand, leaving some for texture. Hose off, and remove leaves with your fingers; some leaves may need to dry for 2 to 3 weeks in order to remove them.

4 place If you embedded objects in the mixture, hose off the excess sand; the objects will remain in the masonry. Set the stones on top of soil or mulch. To lay stones across a lawn, place the stones even with the soil surface so they do not interfere with mowing.

ultimate yard & garden | **75**

garden paths: a melange

dirt path

right: Firmly packed soil creates a path that blends in with the borders on each side. When you make the path, use a tamping tool to pack down the soil; subsequent foot traffic will keep it firm. Pitch the path to one side so water does not collect in the middle after rain. Weeds will have a difficult time germinating in the compacted soil, but you may want to run over it occasionally with a scuffle hoe to eliminate those that do grow.

planting pockets

below left: When laying a path, leave space between some of the stones or pavers to plant creeping or low-growing plants. You can plant a charming herb garden in this fashion; try the Mediterranean herbs—sage, rosemary, lavender, and oregano—that thrive in warmth and well-drained soil.

colorful stepping-stones

below right: For special spots in a garden bed, turn precast cement rounds into decorative art with pieces of broken tile and ceramic plates. Wear safety glasses while breaking up the material; and be careful handling the pieces because they have sharp edges. Use thin-set mortar to attach pieces to the round, and grout the spaces in between.

ever green

above: Grass, cut short, is a classic material for a path. Sod makes a neat walkway that is soft underfoot and its green hues set off the colors in the surrounding garden beds. Edge the path so the sod does not invade the beds—ordinary plastic or rubber edging is fine if you hide it by fronting it with courses of stone or brick or lengths of lumber.

woodland path

left: A gravel path blends in with this forestlike setting as it follows a sinuous trail through plantings of foxgloves, ajuga, ferns, and a towering viburnum. Keep the gravel from spilling into the borders with an edging of local stones or timber. In this kind of woodland design, pine needles and shredded bark would be equally suitable alternatives to the gravel.

fences for gardens

picking a style

Usually garden fences are part of the design of the bed or border. They are chosen more for their aesthetic appeal than privacy. If you want privacy and security, however, you can have an attractive surround. Board-on-board, grapestakes, woven boards, lath, bamboo, and chain link are just a few choices. Improve on chain link by planting vines to climb up and camouflage it. Wood fences have almost unlimited

classic pickets

right: A picket fence is surely one of the best and most traditional choices for showing off your garden. Painted white or left natural to weather to a silvery gray, a picket fence will mark boundaries without completely obstructing the view from either side. The pickets and posts can have plain, pointed, or rounded tops or fancy scrollwork and cutouts.

design and pattern possibilities.

Use a picket fence to enclose a part of the yard—around a cutting or vegetable garden, or an entry or foundation garden. Add a ready-made arbor over the gate for a clematis or a climbing rose.

basics

If you plan to build the fence yourself, check on zoning and permit requirements first.

All fences need sturdy support. With all but split rail, you should secure the posts in cement. You can sink posts for split rails directly into the soil.

perennials

1 daylily, page 115

2 lupine, page 118

3 rose campion, page 118

4 checkerbloom, page 123

5 chrysanthemum, page 111

6 iris, pages 130–131

other plants

a rose

b petunia

c chocolate mint

rustic country style

above: The friendly, open design of a split-rail fence borders a mixed planting of alliums, columbines, daisies, and foxgloves. The mortise-and-tenon fence will easily follow contours or zigzags.

victorian picket

right: A garden of delphiniums and poppies sparkles against the carved white pickets of this stylish fence. If you have a band saw, you can enjoy shaping the tops of the pickets yourself.

elegant wrought iron

left: Jackman clematis climbs, twines, and tumbles over an arbor and wrought-iron fence. Open fencing—with or without a gate—is the perfect support for other climbers as well, such as roses, morning glories, moonflowers, English and Boston ivy, and trumpet vine. Wrought-iron fencing is available prefabricated, which can make installation a do-it-yourself job. Wooden posts are usually set into concrete for stability.

modern openwork

below: To mark a boundary, with no thought of privacy, you can erect a framework of 2x4s with a gridwork of lattice. Such a fence is equally useful for climbing plants—even a wisteria, if you anchor the frame securely into the ground—and for delineating a bed in a flower or vegetable garden. The stepped design here adapts to level or sloping ground.

the
basics

getting started 84

planning & design 86

planting 88

maintenance 90

multiplying plants 92

decorative ornaments 94

seasonal checklist 98

getting started

begin with the soil

The success with gardening depends on the soil. This is especially true with perennials because they may remain in the same place for years. You need to improve the soil before planting. If you have good loam (not too much clay or sand), you should dig the area to a depth of 8 to 12 inches, removing large stones and weeds. Work compost into the top 3 to 4 inches.

fixing it up

If you have less than ideal soil, improve its tilth and moisture-holding ability by spreading a 2-inch layer of peat moss or compost on top of the soil and digging it in. Such amendments help sandy soil particles hold together and clay particles separate, so the former soil will release water more slowly and the latter will allow water to percolate through instead of collecting.

clay soil Soil with a lot of clay in it drains slowly but is high in nutrients. You can form a ball in your hand with clay soil; often the clay structure is not apparent until you have dug down 6 inches or more. If you think you could make bricks with your soil, it has a preponderance of clay.

loam The best soil type you can have is loam. It contains clay, sand, and silt in balanced proportions, along with humus. Humus, which is sometimes called black earth, is the result of decaying vegetable matter in the soil. It is fertile and makes up a good part of loam.

sandy soil Sandy soil is fine and porous. Water passes through this type of soil too easily. That is why it contains and holds few nutrients. The addition of peat moss will help the soil structure. Digging in aged manure and compost will raise its nutrient level.

1 prepare Lay out the shape of the garden bed with stakes and string to establish a pleasing shape and size. Slide a spade under the existing lawn to free it from the soil. If it is healthy turf, remove it in long segments, a spade-width across; roll it up as you remove it. Use the turf to patch areas of the lawn that might need attention.

2 amend Use a garden fork to break up the soil in the bed to a depth of at least 12 inches. Add at least 2 inches of organic matter (compost, leaf mold, well-rotted manure) to the exposed soil to improve its texture, drainage, and ability to retain moisture. Dig or fork it into the top 10 inches. This is the perfect time to add granular slow-acting fertilizer, if you wish.

3 rake Rake the soil smooth. Remove small stones. Break up clods or lumps of soil with the back of a steel rake. Make the bed as level as possible to ensure even distribution of rainwater.

add mulch

After you have planted your garden, spread a 3- to 4-inch layer of mulch over the soil. Use any mulch that is readily available, such as shredded fir bark, wood chips, compost, or seed hulls. (Cocoa bean hulls are fragrant, brown, attractive, and expensive; if you cannot resist them, use them in a small area, such as an herb garden, or top off a less expensive mulch with a thin layer of the hulls.)

Mulch helps the soil stay cool and retain moisture in hot weather. A thick layer also cuts down on weeds, preventing the seeds from germinating. You will find it easier to pull out weeds that germinate in the mulch (from seeds deposited courtesy of the wind or birds), because they will root in the loose mulch, not in the soil.

Mulch plants in late fall to protect them from the alternate freezing and thawing of the soil in winter.

planning & design

thinking ahead

right: Perennials, unlike annuals, do not bloom for months, or even a month, at a time. In deciding what to plant where, the plant's growth habit, foliage texture, shape, and season of bloom are as important as the colors of the flowers.

site selection

opposite top: If you plant a border or bed in full sun, you will have the largest choice of plants. Full sun means at least six hours of direct, unobstructed sun daily. In zones 8 to 11, most perennials appreciate some shade from the hot midday sun.

Place a garden anywhere—in front of a fence or hedge, by a patio or porch, along a walk or driveway, in the center of a lawn. For a country look, you might want to enclose it with a picket fence. For a formal look, surround it with a low-growing hedge, such as boxwood, or private, high-growing hedge of privet or yew.

color palettes

bottom left: Monochromatic gardens can be beautiful, but a garden of mixed colors can be far more interesting. Use contrast (blue fleabane with yellow coreopsis, for example) and harmony (pink poppies with rose coralbells) to create exciting combinations.

design pointers

below: Mix foliage types: spiky, feathery, strap-shape, grasslike, round, and heart-shape. A garden with only one type of foliage won't look as interesting, especially when the plants are not in bloom.

Use plants in odd-numbered groups and repeat the groups at intervals throughout the garden. A group is at least three plants of one variety. When using large plants, such as crambe or gunnera, one plant is sufficient.

When you plant a border, graduate heights from shortest at the edge to tallest in the rear, but be flexible. A few surprises lend variety. For example, a group of foxgloves in the middle or even at a front corner will appear to have seeded itself there (and it may have!). In a bed that is visible from all sides plant the tallest perennials in the center.

Use the aromatic plants. The most fragrant perennials include beebalm, bugbane, dames rocket, iris, peony, phlox, dianthus, and violets.

planting

starting out: year one

above: Even if you have drawn your garden design on paper—and you should have—you may want to make minor adjustments when you get the plants. Set the potted plants on top of the bed and rearrange them until you are sure you like the placement. Then unpot and plant them, spacing them according to their mature size. You can fill bare spots with annuals for the first year or two.

reaping the rewards: year two

right: Starting with nursery stock in large containers will give you a lush garden by the second year. Some plants, such as foxglove and hollyhock, are biennials, which produce foliage the first year, flowers the second. Others—sedum, phlox, peonies—require two to three years to reach their full blooming potential. Many will reseed, giving you an easy way to increase the colorful palette of your garden. If you start with small plants, continue to tuck annuals among them to fill the intervening spaces. Mulch well so that weeds do not have a chance to germinate on the bare soil.

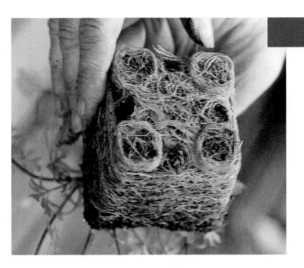

1 unpot Prepare the soil and planting holes before you unpot the plants, so that the roots do not dry out. Water the pots one day prior to planting, to encourage as much soil as possible to cling to the root ball when you tap it out of the pot. A plant that has been growing in the pot too long will have roots encircling the soil, *left*.

2 tease When the plant is out of the pot, gently tease some of the roots, especially the bottom roots, away from the soil ball. If the pot holds multiple plants, use your fingers to separate the individual plants by gently pulling apart the roots.

Set the plants into the ground at the same depth or just slightly deeper than they were growing in the pot. Burying the crown (where stems meet roots) under too much soil can promote crown rot, which will kill the plant.

3 space Space plants at the distance their mature size will require. When you plant a groundcover, however, you may want to space the plants closer together for faster overall coverage. The usual method is to set out the plants in a W-shape pattern. Envision a plant at each of the points in the W. Set plants that increase by means of runners, such as pachysandra and sweet woodruff, slightly farther apart.

maintenance

1 **grooming** To keep the garden attractive all season, remove dead flowers and damaged, diseased, or dead foliage on a regular basis. A few perennials like daylilies, delphiniums, coralbells, and centaurea will produce additional flowering stems over a period of months if you are diligent about cutting off spent blooms. Do not compost diseased foliage; throw it into the trash.

You might want to leave some seedheads on plants to ripen. Collect the seeds (of species or open-pollinated perennials) to sow in the fall or the following spring. Leave the seedheads of asters, black-eyed Susans, coneflowers, and ornamental grasses; they provide food for birds in fall and winter.

2 **watering** Some watering devices are best used as garden ornaments. Old-fashioned sprinklers and fancy ones, such as this alligator, are best for watering the lawn or ornamenting the perennial garden. Most plants will be healthier if you do not wet the foliage. This is particularly true for phlox, beebalm, and other perennials that have a tendency to suffer from mildew.

3 **tip-top tools** Keep your tools in good shape. After each use, wipe off any soil that sticks to the head and dip the head into a bucket of sand to which you have added clean motor oil. Scour off rust with sandpaper. Put the tools in a designated space where they are kept clean and dry.

water wise No matter where you live, be conservative about water use. Water wisely with drip irrigation using a system of emitters, soaker hoses, or in-line sprinklers. The water gets right to the plants' roots instead of wasted through evaporation. Plants need at least 1 inch of water weekly from rain or from a hose.

4

winter protection Unless you live in a warm-winter zone, provide some protection from the cold and from the alternate freezing and thawing of the soil. You can use prunings from evergreen trees or a 3- to 4-inch layer of mulch, such as wood chips or straw. Wait until after the first hard freeze to apply winter mulch. Remove mulch gradually in spring as the air and soil warm. (The exception is early-blooming perennials, such as hellebores, Virginia bluebells, and Dutchman's breeches; pull back mulch from them in late winter or early spring.)

5

mulch Save time and effort when you weed and water by putting down a 3- to 4-inch layer of mulch, such as shredded wood or bark, in late spring. Weed seeds will not germinate readily without light; wind- or animal-borne weeds that appear are easy to pull up because they root in the mulch, not in the soil. The soil will retain moisture longer with a covering of mulch.

6

multiplying plants

why divide

There are many reasons for dividing plants (digging them up, separating them into sections, and then replanting) aside from the desire to have more of your favorites to spread around the garden. Although you can leave some perennials, such as peonies, undisturbed for decades, you will find that most plants benefit from being divided after spending three or more years in one place.

How do you know when you need to divide a plant? Look for these signs: The plant seems crowded, it produces fewer or smaller blooms than usual, or the center of the plant looks woody or browned.

Another reason for obtaining new plants by division instead of starting from seeds, cuttings, or layering is that division is easy to do and gives you plants that will usually bloom the same year.

dividing fibrous-rooted perennials

dig Before you divide a plant, dig the holes into which you will put the new divisions, so the roots will not dry out. With a garden spade, dig deep around and under the plant (a daylily, *right*), keeping as much of the root ball intact as possible.

divide Separate the clump into two or more sections (with roots) by slicing them apart with a sharp knife, cutting them with a spade (as with the coreopsis, *right*), or prying them apart with two garden forks placed back to back. Some perennials (sundrops, yarrow, and bugleweed, for example) produce rosettes from roots that grow around the edge of the plant; it is easy to cut off these rooted rosettes.

replant Remove dead or damaged roots from the division and cut back foliage by one-half to two-thirds. Plant immediately and water well. Some plants have special planting-depth requirements. Peonies, *right*, will not bloom or will take one to two years to flower if you set the roots deeper than 2 inches below the surface. Replant most perennials, however, at the same depth they were originally growing.

1 dividing iris

dig Dig up the crowded plants and wash off some of the dirt to expose new shoots and the rhizome to which they are attached. Break or cut apart the new rhizomes from the old clump.

2 divide Make sure each new rhizome has one or two leaf fans. Discard the oldest, woody rhizomes and any that show signs of disease or damage.

Trim back the foliage by about two-thirds (to 5 inches) to compensate for the smaller number of roots. Before replanting, you can dip the rhizomes in sulfur powder to prevent mold.

3 plant Set the rhizomes 3 to 4 inches apart in shallow trenches, roots downward. Position them so all the leaf fans face the same direction (outward, or the direction in which you want them to grow). Cover the roots and about half of the rhizome with soil. Water well.

all in the timing

Divide most perennials in spring, just as new growth is beginning. If you live in the Deep South, divide in fall when the weather is cooler and wetter. It is easier to divide plants that do not have a lot of top growth. If they do, cut back the foliage by at least half, either before you dig them up or as you replant them.

No matter what the zone, propagate peonies in late summer to fall, when their roots make the most growth. Divide iris in late summer, and spring-blooming perennials right after they have finished flowering.

Some plants grow best (healthier and with excellent flower production if you divide them every one to two years. These include artemisia, New England aster, boltonia, chrysanthemum, Helen's flower, Joe-Pye weed, michaelmas daisy, primrose, black-eyed Susan, snow-in-summer, yarrow, and yellow loosestrife.

decorative ornaments

finishing touches

Ornaments direct visitors' attention to or away from an area. Decorative objects can camouflage the sparseness of a new planting. They can be delightful surprises hidden among lush, mature perennials.

Artful plaques, small statues and even pyramid-shape piles of stones placed along the curve of a path can point the way to another garden bed.

Sculptures, obelisks, and fountains provide vertical accents in gardens that lack surrounding trees,

express yourself

right: Every garden is an expression of its owner's personality, from the shape and size of the bed to the colors of the plants and the design of paths and trellises. The ornaments you use to accent your perennial beds and borders are part of that expression, whether exuberant—like the playful items in this garden—or subtle.

trellises, walls, climbing vines, or other vertical components.

Select an item as a focal point instead of as an accent. Sundials, birdbaths, or even a bird feeder on a pole can easily be the center of attention in a garden. Any of these would be attractive in a country-style or naturalistic planting. For shade gardens, which tend to resemble woodlands, choose unobtrusive accents such as stonelike statues and wood sculpture.

Weather vanes and kinetic sculptures lend a sense of movement even when there is none; they are especially enjoyable on hot, windless summer days. As much as possible, select ornaments that you can leave in the garden year-round.

careful selection

below: Choose decorative objects that complement the style of your garden. Cute rabbits or frogs, for instance, would look inappropriate in a formal garden edged with boxwood, whereas this gazing ball, a sundial, or armillary sphere are suitable.

ultimate yard & garden | **95**

display collections
above: Whatever your interest or hobby, indulge it to accent your garden, but do so with a bit of prudence.

fabulous finds
above right: A devotee of flea markets? Use your finds in unique ways, as in this hockey stick arbor.

flock with them
right: Love flamingos? Set them in a natural-looking group. Use their color to reflect the plantings—bleeding hearts and tulips.

special care

left: Although most ornaments sold for garden use are weatherproof, you will need to bring those that are not indoors to a basement or garage for winter in zones with freezing temperatures. Ceramic and concrete accessories may crack in temperatures below freezing. Others, like this statuesque crane, may be too fragile or valuable to be left outdoors to withstand the rigors of northern winters.

well-aged

below: Materials such as copper, iron, wood, and resin are, for the most part, impervious to rain and cold. The copper in the base of the sundial takes on a lovely shade of verdigris as it ages. Woods, such as redwood and cedar, turn silvery gray over the years.

ultimate yard & garden | **97**

seasonal checklist

	Spring	Summer

Cool Climates

Spring
- Begin to pull back winter mulch from perennial beds.
- Fertilize plants in beds and borders as new growth begins to emerge.
- Divide crowded or old clumps of summer- and fall-blooming perennials.
- Stake or support perennials that tend to get floppy before they grow too tall.
- Dig new garden beds; enlarge existing ones.
- Install drip irrigation.
- Set new plants into gardens. Water them thoroughly as soon as they are in place.
- Cut back flowering stems on bulbs as blooms fade; leave foliage to mature.

Summer
- Fill in vacant spots in the garden with annuals for continuous color.
- In early summer, divide perennials that bloomed in spring, except for iris and peonies. Divide those in late summer.
- Deadhead spent blooms to encourage more flowers later in the season.
- Mulch bare soil between plants to help retain moisture and prevent weeds.
- Inspect plants regularly for pests. Hose off aphids. Knock Japanese beetles into a jar of soapy water.
- Inspect plants for powdery mildew; spray regularly with an organic fungicide.
- Tuck errant stems of climbing vines into trellises, or prune them off.

Warm Climates

Spring
- Mulch bare soil between plants to help retain moisture and prevent weeds.
- Fill in vacant spots in the garden with annuals for continuous color.
- Install drip irrigation.
- Dig new garden beds; enlarge existing ones.
- Tuck errant stems of climbing vines into trellises, or prune them off.
- Inspect plants for pests. Hose off aphids. Knock Japanese beetles into a jar filled with soapy water.
- Plant container-grown perennials.

Summer
- Deadhead spent blooms to encourage more flowers later in the season.
- Water newly planted perennials regularly during dry spells.
- Divide bearded iris in late summer.
- Collect seeds of poppies, daylilies, and columbine to sow in fall.
- Inspect plants for powdery mildew; spray regularly with an organic fungicide.

Fall

- ☐ After a hard frost, cut back dead flower and foliage stems to within a few inches of the soil. Leave the plumes on ornamental grasses and the seedheads on coneflowers, black-eyed Susans, and other plants that provide food for winter birds.
- ☐ Plant new perennials such as peonies, chrysanthemums, and asters.
- ☐ Spread winter mulch over perennial beds after the ground freezes hard. Use several inches of straw, chopped leaves, or evergreen boughs.
- ☐ Build new compost bins or repair old ones. Turn and consolidate compost piles.
- ☐ Take a soil test while the ground is still workable.
- ☐ Plant spring-flowering bulbs for early color in perennial beds.

Winter

- ☐ If the ground hasn't frozen yet, finish planting bulbs that were overlooked during the fall.
- ☐ Make a list of perennials that will need dividing in spring.
- ☐ Look through mail-order catalogs and order plants for early- to late-spring arrival.
- ☐ Keep watering newly planted perennials as long as the ground is not frozen.
- ☐ After the holidays, cut up the Christmas tree and lay the boughs over any tender perennials.

- ☐ Plant pansies, calendulas, and primroses for fall and winter color.
- ☐ Deadhead and maintain the area around cool-season annuals such as larkspur.
- ☐ Divide overly large and overcrowded perennials to control size and promote next year's blooming.
- ☐ Plant new perennials.
- ☐ Cut back dead flower and foliage stems to within a few inches of the soil.
- ☐ Continue to remove weeds, especially perennial weeds.
- ☐ Keep lightweight fabric handy to cover and protect annuals from light frosts.

- ☐ Cut back chrysanthemums as they finish blooming; sidedress with fertilizer.
- ☐ Build new compost bins or repair old ones. Turn and consolidate compost piles to prepare for the new season.
- ☐ Prune and spray hybrid tea roses with dormant oil prior to leaf bud break. If leaves are out, use light (superior) oil.
- ☐ Protect perennials from heavy frost by covering them with a bed sheet, polyspun garden fabric, or a makeshift tent of plastic (with ventilation holes).

the
plants

common and botanical names 102
perennial plants 106
ferns 126
grasses 128
iris 130

common and botanical names

common name	botanical name
aeonium	*Aeonium* species
allium	*Allium* species and cultivars
artemisia	*Artemisia* species and cultivars
aster	*Aster* species and cultivars
astilbe	*Astilbe × arendsii*
aubretia	*Aubretia × deltoidea*
baby's breath	*Gypsophila paniculata*
balloon flower	*Platycodon grandiflorus*
bamboo	*Pleioblastus* species
baptisia	*Baptisia australis*
barrenwort	*Epimedium* species and cultivars
bearded iris	*Iris germanica*
beard-tongue	*Penstemon* species and cultivars
beebalm	*Monarda* species and cultivars
bellflower	*Campanula* species and cultivars
bergenia	*Bergenia ciliata*
black-eyed Susan	*Rudbeckia* species and cultivars
blazing star	*Liatris spicata*
bleeding heart	*Dicentra spectabilis*
blue false indigo	*Baptisia australis*
blue fescue	*Festuca glauca*
blue flag	*Iris versicolor*
blue oat grass	*Helictotrichon sempervirens*
blue star	*Amsonia tabernaemontana*
boltonia	*Boltonia asteroides*
bouncing bet	*Saponaria ocymoides*
bowles golden sedge	*Carex stricta* 'Bowles Golden'
brunnera	*Brunnera macrophylla*
butterfly weed	*Asclepias tuberosa*
candytuft	*Iberis sempervirens*
canterbury bells	*Campanula* species and cultivars
cardinal flower	*Lobelia cardinalis*
carolina lupine	*Thermopsis villosa*
catmint	*Nepeta × faassenii*
chamomile	*Chamaemelum nobile*
checkerbloom	*Sidalcea malviflora*
cholla	*Opuntia* species and cultivars
christmas fern	*Polystichum acrostichoides*
chrysanthemum	*Chrysanthemum* cultivars
cinnamon fern	*Osmunda cinnamomea*
clematis	*Clematis* species and cultivars
colewort	*Crambe cordifolia*
columbine	*Aquilegia* species and cultivars
coralbells	*Heuchera* species and cultivars
coreopsis	*Coreopsis* species and cultivars

corydalis . . . . *Corydalis lutea*
crambe . . . . *Crambe cordifolia*
cranesbill . . . . *Geranium* species and cultivars
creeping myrtle . . . . *Vinca minor*
crested iris . . . . *Iris cristata*
crested wood fern . . . . *Dryopteris cristata*
cushion spurge . . . . *Euphorbia polychroma*
dalmation iris . . . . *Iris pallida*
daylily . . . . *Hemerocallis* species and cultivars
dead nettle . . . . *Lamium* species and cultivars
delphinium . . . . *Delphinium* cultivars
dianthus . . . . *Dianthus* species and cultivars
dittany . . . . *Dictamnus albus*
epimedium . . . . *Epimedium* species and cultivars
false goatsbeard . . . . *Astilbe × arendsii*
false sunflower . . . . *Heliopsis helianthoides*
feather reed grass . . . . *Calamagrostis acutiflora* 'Stricta'
feverfew . . . . *Tanacetum parthenium*
flowering onion . . . . *Allium* species and cultivars
foamflower . . . . *Tiarella cordifolia*
fountain grass . . . . *Pennisetum alopecuroides*
foxglove . . . . *Digitalis purpurea*
garden phlox . . . . *Phlox paniculata*
gas plant . . . . *Dictamnus albus*
gayfeather . . . . *Liatris spicata*
goatsbeard . . . . *Aruncus dioicus*
goldenrod . . . . *Solidago* species and cultivars
greek valerian . . . . *Polemonium caeruleum*
greek windflower . . . . *Anemone blanda*
hakone grass . . . . *Hakonechloa macra*
hardy begonia . . . . *Begonia grandis* ssp. *evansiana*
hardy cyclamen . . . . *Cyclamen hederifolium*
hardy ice plant . . . . *Delosperma cooperi*
harebell . . . . *Campanula* species and cultivars
hay-scented fern . . . . *Dennstaedtia punctilobula*
hedgehog cactus . . . . *Pediocactus simpsonii* var. *minor*
hellebore . . . . *Helleborus* species and cultivars
holly fern . . . . *Cyrtomium falcatum*
hollyhock . . . . *Alcea rosea*
hosta . . . . *Hosta* species and culitvars
ivy . . . . *Hedera* species and cultivars
jacob's ladder . . . . *Polemonium caeruleum*
japanese blood grass . . . . *Imperata cylindrica* 'Red Baron'
japanese iris . . . . *Iris ensata*
japanese painted fern . . . . *Athyrium nipponicum* 'Pictum'
joe-pye weed . . . . *Eupatorium maculatum*

common and botanical names

jupiter's beard . . . . *Centranthus ruber*
kalimeris . . . . *Kalimeris pinnatifida*
knautia . . . . *Knautia macedonica*
lamb's ears . . . . *Stachys byzantina*
lamium . . . . *Lamium* species and cultivars
lavender cotton . . . . *Santolina chamaecyparissus*
leopard plant . . . . *Ligularia* species and cultivars
leopard's bane . . . . *Doronicum caucasium*
lily . . . . *Lilium* species and cultivars
lily-of-the-valley . . . . *Convallaria majalis*
lilyturf . . . . *Liriope* species and cultivars
louisiana iris . . . . *Iris* hybrids
lungwort . . . . *Pulmonaria* species and cultivars
lupine . . . . *Lupinus* cultivars
maidenhair fern . . . . *Adiantum pedatum*
marguerite . . . . *Leucanthemum vulgare*
marsh marigold . . . . *Caltha palustris*
meadow buttercup . . . . *Ranunculus acris*
meadow rue . . . . *Thalictrum* species and cultivars
mexican hat . . . . *Ratibida columnifera*
milfoil . . . . *Achillea* species and cultivars
miniature hollyhock . . . . *Sidalcea malviflora*
monkshood . . . . *Aconitum carmichaelii*
montbretia . . . . *Crocosmia* species and cultivars
moss phlox . . . . *Phlox subulata*
mountain pink . . . . *Phlox subulata*
mugwort . . . . *Artemisia* species and cultivars
mullein . . . . *Verbascum* species and cultivars
navelwort . . . . *Omphaloides cappadocica*
omphaloides . . . . *Omphaloides cappadocica*
oriental poppy . . . . *Papaver orientale*
orris . . . . *Iris pallida*
ostrich fern . . . . *Matteuccia struthiopteris*
ox-eye daisy . . . . *Leucanthemum vulgare*
pampas grass . . . . *Cortaderia selloana*
peony . . . . *Paeonia lactiflora* and cultivars
periwinkle . . . . *Vinca minor*
pinks . . . . *Dianthus* species and cultivars
prairie coneflower . . . . *Ratibida columnifera*
prickly pear . . . . *Opuntia* species and cultivars
primrose . . . . *Primula* species and cultivars
pulmonaria . . . . *Pulmonaria* species and cultivars
purple coneflower . . . . *Echinacea purpurea*
queen-of-the-prairie . . . . *Filipendula rubra*
red hot poker . . . . *Kniphofia* species and cultivars
red valerian . . . . *Centranthus ruber*

rock rose	*Helianthemum* cultivars
rose campion	*Lychnis coronaria*
rose mallow	*Hibiscus moscheutos*
russian sage	*Perovskia atriplicifolia*
sage	*Salvia* species and cultivars
salvia	*Salvia* species and cultivars
saxifrage	*Saxifraga* species and cultivars
sea pink	*Armeria maritima*
sedum	*Sedum* species and cultivars
sheep's bit	*Jasione laevis*
siberian bugloss	*Brunnera macrophylla*
siberian iris	*Iris sibirica*
snow-in-summer	*Cerastium tomentosum*
soapwort	*Saponaria ocymoides*
solomon's seal	*Polygonatum* species and cultivars
speedwell	*Veronica* species and cultivars
spiderwort	*Tradescantia virginiana*
stone cress	*Aethionema armenum*
stokes' aster	*Stokesia laevis*
summer phlox	*Phlox paniculata*
sundrops	*Oenothera fruticosa*
sun rose	*Helianthemum* cultivars
swamp rose mallow	*Hibiscus moscheutos*
sweet woodruff	*Galium odoratum*
switch grass	*Panicum virgatum*
thrift	*Armeria maritima*
thyme	*Thymus* species and cultivars
tickseed	*Coreopsis* species and cultivars
toadlily	*Tricyrtis* species and cultivars
torchlily	*Kniphofia* species and cultivars
tree peony	*Paeonia suffruticosa*
trillium	*Trillium* species and cultivars
trumpet vine	*Campsis radicans*
turtlehead	*Chelone glabra*
variegated italian arum	*Arum italicum* 'Pictum'
veronica	*Veronica* species and cultivars
vervain	*Verbena* species and cultivars
wake-robin	*Trillium* species and cultivars
wild ginger	*Asarum canadense*
wild sweet william	*Phlox divaricata*
willow amsonia	*Amsonia tabernaemontana*
yarrow	*Achillea* species and cultivars
yellowbells	*Kirengeshoma palmata*
yellow flag	*Iris pseudacorus*
yellow loosestrife	*Lysimachia punctata*
zebra grass	*Miscanthus sinensis* 'Zebrinus'

Achillea species and cultivars
yarrow (milfoil)
2'–4' tall
Pink, rose, red, white, pale yellow blooms
Flowers summer to fall
Sun
Zones 3–9
Use in border, butterfly, container, or cutting
gardens

Feathery, grayish green foliage and flat-topped clusters of flowers add texture and airy accents to borders. Easy to grow; needs good drainage; drought-tolerant.

Aconitum carmichaelii
monkshood
3'–6' tall
Deep blue to purple blooms
Flowers mid- to late summer
Partial sun to light shade
Zones 4–8
Use in border gardens

Desirable for its deep color in late summer. Deeply cut leaves are attractive all season. All parts of the plant, including the blossoms, are *very* poisonous; **do not plant if you have curious young children.**

Aeonium species
aeonium
6"–10" tall
Yellow, white, red blooms
Flowers spring
Sun
Zones 9–11
Use in border, container, and Xeriscape
gardens

Much appreciated for its rosettes of leaves. Use as a specimen planting or mix with other plants. 'Zwartkopf' with its deep burgundy leaves makes a bold garden statement.

perennial plants

Aethionema armenum
stone cress
8"–12" tall
Pink, white blooms
Flowers late spring
Sun
Zones 6–9
Use in border, container, and rock gardens

Tufts of grayish green leaves covered with flowers in spring. Needs good drainage. Shear after blooms fade to keep looking neat. 'Warley Rose' is a beautiful interspecific cross with blue-gray leaves tinted red, and dark pink flowers striped with light pink veins.

Alcea rosea
hollyhock
4'–8' tall
Pink, rose, red, purple, white, pale yellow blooms
Flowers summer to late summer
Sun
Zones 3–9
Use in border gardens

Wonderfully showy, old-fashioned plant for the back of the border. Single- and double-flowered cultivars available: Powderpuff Hybrids, 'Chater's Double'. Actually a biennial that self-seeds, so seems perennial. Not long-lived. Transplant seedlings in spring.

Allium species
allium (flowering onion)
1'–3' tall
Fragrant pink, lilac, blue, yellow, white blooms
Flowers late spring to early summer
Sun
Zones 4–9
Use in border, container, cutting, and edible
gardens

Hundreds of species, including chives (*A. schoenoprasum*), which look as good edging a border as they do in an herb garden. Other ornamental alliums range from petite, yellow *A. moly* to lilac-blue *A. christophii*, with its gigantic globular flower, and rosy purple *A. pulchellum*, which has loose, pendulous florets. Alliums may self-sow but not invasively.

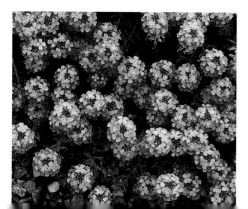

Amsonia tabernaemontana
blue star (willow amsonia)
2'–3' tall
Slate blue blooms
Flowers late spring to early summer
Sun to light shade
Zones 5–9
Use in border and naturalistic gardens

Native to North America. Star-shape flowers add sparkle to lightly shaded gardens. Easy to grow; self-sows prolifically. Combines well with coreopsis, blue false indigo, iris, and low-growing phlox.

Armeria maritima
sea pink (thrift)
4"–10" tall
Pink, red, white blooms
Flowers late spring to early summer
Sun
Zones 3–9
Use in border, rock, and wild gardens

Grassy leaves and bright flowers. Good as an edging at the front of a border or popping up among rocks. Good groundcover. Attracts hummingbirds. Easy to grow. 'Alba' is white.

Anemone blanda
greek windflower
6" tall
Blue, mauve, pink, white blooms
Flowers spring
Light shade
Zones 5–8
Use in border, container, and wild gardens, and as a groundcover

Delightful, daisy-like flowers and divided leaves. Creates a carpet of color under deciduous trees. Easy to grow. Spreads slowly in soil with good drainage. Does not require division, although that is a good way to increase the plants. There are many cultivars.

Artemisia species and cultivars
artemisia (mugwort)
1'–2' tall
Silver-gray; fragrant leaves; insignificant blooms
Flowers summer
Sun
Zones 4–9
Use in border, container, and cutting gardens and as a groundcover

Beautiful, feathery foliage plant for midborder. Some are native to North America. Spreads, sometimes aggressively, by underground runners. 'Silver Mound' is more restrained than 'Silver King' and 'Silver Queen'.

Aquilegia species and cultivars
columbine
1½'–2' tall
Red, blue, yellow, white, and bicolor blooms
Flowers late spring to early summer
Sun
Zones 3–9
Use in border, container, and wild gardens

Native to North America. Large-flowered McKana Hybrids and compact and long-spurred Music Hybrids are excellent strains. Graceful plants for the front of borders. Not long-lived but self-sows freely.

Arum italicum 'Pictum'
variegated italian arum
12"–18" tall
Greenish yellow- or white-margined leaves; purple blooms
Flowers late spring to early summer
Partial sun to light shade
Zones 4–9
Use in shade gardens, and as a groundcover

Dark green marbled foliage appears in fall, persists through winter, disappears in late spring. Clusters of orange-red berries last for weeks. Combines well with creeping phlox.

Aruncus dioicus
goatsbeard
3'–4½' tall
White, cream blooms with unpleasant fragrance
Flowers late spring to summer
Sun to light shade
Zones 6–9
Use in borders and wild gardens

An imposing plant because of its size.
Feathery, 12-inch-long plumes lend an airy
aspect. Good at rear of borders or near trees.
Combines well with ornamental grasses.

Asarum canadense
wild ginger
5"–8" tall
Purple-brown, inconspicuous blooms
Flowers spring
Light shade to shade
Zones 4–8
Use in naturalistic gardens, and as a groundcover

Native to North America. Deciduous heart-shape
leaves. Other species are evergreen—*A. virginicum*
(hardy to Zone 7), *A. europaeum* European ginger
(hardy to Zone 5). Combines well with sweet
woodruff, hellebore, and epimedium.

Asclepias tuberosa
butterfly weed
2'–3' tall
Fragrant orange, yellow, pink, vermilion blooms
Flowers summer
Sun
Zones 3–9
Use in border, butterfly, and container
    gardens

A must-have native that attracts butterflies.
Drought-tolerant. Slow to emerge in spring; be
careful not to dig up the roots. Colorful flower
clusters. Easy to grow; pest- and disease-free.

perennial plants

Aster species and cultivars
aster
2' tall
Blue blooms
Flowers late summer to fall
Sun
Zones 4–9
Use in border, butterfly, and wild gardens

Very long-blooming. Another excellent cultivar
is 'Wonder of Staffa' (lavender-blue). *A. novae-
angliae* (New England aster) and *A. novi-belgii*
(Michaelmas daisy) are native to North
America, with scores of cultivars and colors
from white and pink to red and claret.

Astilbe x *arendsii*
astilbe (false goatsbeard)
2'–3' tall
Pink, rose, red, white blooms
Flowers early summer
Partial sun to shade
Zones 5–8
Use in border, container, and cutting gardens

Finely divided foliage makes plant attractive
even without its flowers. Does not grow well
in areas with hot, humid summers. Combines
well with hostas, hellebores, and ferns.

Aubretia x *deltoidea*
aubretia
6"–9" tall
Mauve, magenta, rose, pink, white blooms
Flowers late spring
Sun to light shade
Zones 4–8
Use in border, container, and rock gardens;
    and as a groundcover

Mat-forming evergreen plant with long-lasting
single or double blooms. Prefers sandy soil,
good drainage. Cut off spent blooms to keep
plant compact. Hybrids include 'Borsch's White',
'Purple Gem', and *A. deltoidea* 'Variegata' (blue
flowers, silvery white-edged foliage).

Baptisia australis
baptisia (blue false indigo)
2'-3' tall
Deep blue blooms
Flowers late spring to summer
Sun
Zones 4-8
Use in border and naturalistic gardens

Lupine-like flowers. There are several species that bear white blossoms. *Baptisia lactea* blooms in spring and *B. leucantha* is hardy to Zone 3. *B. tinctoria* is a yellow-flowered species.

Boltonia asteroides
boltonia
4'-5' tall
White, pink, purple, violet blooms
Flowers late summer
Sun
Zones 3-9
Use in border and cutting gardens

White-flowered 'Snowbank' is a lovely, vigorous cultivar. 'Nana' (a cultivar of *B.* var. *latisquama*, a southeastern American native plant) is 3 feet tall. Combines well with fountain grass, asters, and Russian sage.

Begonia grandis
hardy begonia
1½'-2½' tall
Fragrant pink blooms
Flowers summer
Partial sun to light shade
Zones 7-10
Use in borders, containers, and as a groundcover

Angel-wing-shape leaves are red beneath; reddish stems. Forms bulblets in leaf axils; keep them in dry peat moss over winter and plant in spring. 'Alba' has white flowers. Adds a charming, light touch to the garden.

Brunnera macrophylla
brunnera (siberian bugloss)
8"-18" tall
Bright blue blooms
Flowers late spring
Light shade
Zones 3-9
Use in borders and as a groundcover

Forget-me-not-like flowers. With sufficient moisture, grows in sun as well as shade. Easy to grow. Variegated cultivars ('Hadspen Cream' and 'Variegata') need protection from sun and wind to prevent burning. Self-seeds freely.

Bergenia ciliata
bergenia
10"-20" tall
Rose, pink, red, white blooms
Flowers midspring
Light shade
Zones 3-9
Use in borders and as a groundcover

Evergreen, usually heart-shape leaves. Prefers moist soil; tolerates dry. Green or burgundy foliage. White blooms of 'Silberlicht' ('Silver Light') become tinted pink as they age.

Caltha palustris
marsh marigold
18" tall
Fragrant yellow blooms
Flowers spring
Light shade
Zones 4-10
Use in border, edible, and naturalistic gardens

Prefers moist sites, near a pond, for example. There are double- and white-flowered forms. Dies to the ground in summer; tuck it where other plants will cover the empty space. Leaves are edible when cooked like spinach.

109

Campanula species and cultivars
bellflower (harebell, canterbury bells)
6"–48" tall
Blue, white blooms
Flowers summer
Sun to light shade
Zones 3–9
Use in border, container, cutting, and rock gardens

From small *C. carpatica* to medium *C. glomerata* and tall *C. latifolia*, bellflowers are showy, easy-care plants. There are many cultivars to suit any color scheme in the blue to white range.

Campsis radicans
trumpet vine
15'–20' tall
Orange, red, yellow blooms
Flowers summer to fall
Sun
Zones 4–10
Use on trellises, arbors; attracts hummingbirds

Native to southeastern North America. Climbs quickly by aerial roots. Very heat- and drought-tolerant. 'Crimson Trumpet' and 'Praecox' have large red blooms; 'Flava', yellow flowers; 'Mme. Galen', apricot.

Centranthus ruber
red valerian (jupiter's beard)
30"–36" tall
Very fragrant crimson to rose blooms
Flowers early to late summer
Sun or light shade
Zones 4–9
Use in border, butterfly, container, and cutting gardens

Easy to grow; readily self-seeds. Shear after flowering to encourage rebloom. Drought-tolerant, but water helps keep the plant from getting woody. 'Albus' has white flowers.

perennial plants

Cerastium tomentosum
snow-in-summer
6"–12" tall
White blooms
Flowers early summer
Sun to light shade
Zones 3–8
Use in container and rock gardens, and as a groundcover

Silvery gray leaves and pure white flowers are eye-catching. Easy to grow; can be invasive; 'Silver Carpet' and 'Yo-Yo' are less so. Shear off spent blooms to keep plant looking neat.

Chamaemelum nobile (Anthemis nobilis)
chamomile
8"–12" tall
Fragrant white daisylike blooms
Flowers late spring through summer
Sun to light shade
Zones 6–9
Use in border and container gardens

Herb with apple-scented flowers on slender stalks. After flowers fade, shear back to encourage reblooming. Used in teas and tisanes. May cause contact dermatitis in susceptible people.

Chelone glabra
turtlehead
2'–3' tall
Rose-white, purple blooms
Flowers mid- to late summer
Sun to light shade
Zones 3–9
Use in borders

Native to North America. Easy to grow in moist soil. Stiff stems make it quite weather-resistant. Related species bloom later, into September including rosy purple *C. obliqua* and pink *C. lyonii*, which cannot take full sun, especially in warm zones.

Chrysanthemum (Dendranthema) cultivars
chrysanthemum
1'–3' tall
All colors (except blue) and bicolor blooms
Flowers late summer through fall
Sun
Zones 4–9
Use in border, container, and cutting gardens

Traditional fall flower. Easy care. Does best when divided every year; discard the older center clump. Flowers vary in size and shape, from small buttons to large dahlia types. Scores of cultivars are available.

Coreopsis species and cultivars
coreopsis (tickseed)
1½'–2½' tall
Bright to pale yellow blooms
Flowers early to midsummer
Sun to light shade
Zones 3–9
Use in border, butterfly, container, and cutting gardens

Dependable, long-blooming native perennial. Single- and double-flowered cultivars. Deadhead for continued flowering. Combines well with any other perennials.

Clematis species and cultivars
clematis
5"–12' tall
Blue, white, pink, purple, red, and bicolor blooms; some are fragrant
Flowers summer to fall
Sun
Zones 3–9, depending on species
Use as a vine for trellises and arbors

Wonderful on an arbor alone or with climbing roses. Fluffy seed heads add long-season interest. The many species and cultivars vary in season of bloom and in height. Plant with roots in shade, tops in sun.

Corydalis lutea
corydalis
9"–12" tall
Yellow blooms
Flowers early spring to late summer
Partial sun to light shade
Zones 5–8
Use in border, rock, and naturalistic gardens

Small flowers resemble those of its relative, bleeding heart. Self-sows readily. Will grow in rock walls and between paving stones as well as at the front of a border. 'Alba' has white flowers. Not bothered by pests or diseases; does not transplant easily.

Convallaria majalis
lily-of-the-valley
6"–8" tall
Fragrant white, pink blooms
Flowers mid- to late spring
Partial sun to shade
Zones 2–9
Use in naturalistic gardens, and as a groundcover

Wonderful, sweet fragrance. Tolerates dry soil but prefers rich, moist soil; competes well with shallow tree roots. Spreads slowly. Combines well with deciduous trees and shrubs.

Crambe cordifolia
crambe (colewort)
2'–6' tall
Fragrant white blooms
Flowers early summer
Sun
Zones 6–9
Use in border gardens, and as a specimen plant

The immense heart-shape leaves are magnificent at the rear of a border in a large garden. Stake the flower stalks. Slugs may be a problem; otherwise, an easy plant to grow if given a lot of space. Birds like the seeds.

111

Crocosmia cultivars
montbretia
3'–3½' tall
Fragrant flame red, yellow, orange, apricot blooms
Flowers midsummer
Sun to light shade
Zones 6–9
Use in border, container, cutting, naturalistic, and hummingbird gardens

One of the better-known cultivars is 'Lucifer', a bigeneric hybrid with flowers that last 3 to 4 weeks. Needs well-drained soil. Mulch well for winter in the North.

Cyclamen hederifolium (*C. neapolitanum*)
hardy cyclamen
3"–4" tall
Fragrant white with crimson eye or pink blooms
Flowers fall
Light shade to medium shade
Zones 6–8
Use in border, container, hillside, and naturalistic gardens

Heart-shape green leaves mottled with silver appear in fall, last through winter, disappear in spring. Leave the plant undisturbed for years; it will spread slowly. Easy to grow in soil with good drainage.

Delosperma cooperi
hardy iceplant
2"–4" tall
Purple–red blooms
Flowers summer to fall
Sun
Zones 6–9
Use in border, Xeriscape, and container gardens, and as a groundcover

Showy plant for Xeriscape gardens. Spreads but not invasively. Requires soil with good drainage. Pest- and disease-free. One of the truly low-maintenance plants. Combines well with cacti and succulents.

perennial plants

Delphinium cultivars
delphinium
3'–6' tall
Fragrant blue, white, pink blooms
Flowers early to midsummer
Sun to light shade
Zones 3–8
Use in border and cutting gardens

Stately, back-of-the-border plant; not long-lived. Stake tall flower stalks; cut back spent stalks for rebloom. Needs alkaline soil. Grows best in cool climates. May be bothered by mildew, black spot, mites, and slugs. Cultivars of the 'Pacific Hybrid' strain are noteworthy.

Dianthus species and cultivars
dianthus (pinks, sweet william)
6"–18" tall
Fragrant pink, rose, red, and white blooms
Flowers late spring to midsummer
Sun to light shade
Zones 4–9
Use in border and cutting gardens

Old-fashioned perennial for the front of a border. Newer cultivars will often rebloom until September if you deadhead spent flowers. Many have evergreen foliage. Provide winter protection in cold zones with a layer of mulch. Cultivars include spring-blooming 'Bath's Pink' (blue-green foliage), everblooming 'Zing Rose', and deep red 'Desmond'.

Dicentra spectabilis
bleeding heart
12"–20" tall
Pink, white blooms
Flowers late spring to early summer
Light shade
Zones 3–9
Use in borders and cutting gardens

Lovely plant for the shade garden. Goes dormant by midsummer; plant with hosta, ferns, and astilbes to disguise the empty space. 'Alba' is a white-flowered cultivar. The foliage of *D. eximia* and *D. formosa* does not die down in summer. Dutchman's breeches, *D. cucullaria*, bears white blooms in early spring.

Dictamnus albus
gas plant (dittany)
2'–4' tall
Fragrant dark purple, pink, white blooms
Flowers early to midsummer
Sun to light shade
Zones 3–8
Use in border gardens

Fairly drought-tolerant. Leaves have a lemon fragrance when crushed (foliage can cause dermatitis; seeds are toxic). 'Purpureus' has mauve blooms; 'Rubra', rosy purple blooms.

Echinacea purpurea
purple coneflower
3'–4' tall
Dark pink blooms with brownish-purple disk
Flowers summer to fall
Sun
Zones 3–9
Use in border, bird, butterfly, container, and
    cutting gardens

Native eastern North American plant. Attracts wildlife. Long bloom season. Drought-tolerant. Many cultivars: purple 'Magnus', pink 'Crimson Star', 18-inch-tall 'White Swan'.

Digitalis purpurea
foxglove
2'–4' tall
Pink, white, purple-spotted blooms
Flowers early to midsummer
Partial sun to light shade
Zones 4–8
Use in border and cutting gardens

Classic plant for the rear of a border. Perfect for a cottage garden. Not long-lived (usually biennial) but self-sows freely. Cut off spent flower stems for a second blooming. The 'Excelsior' and 'Shirley' strains have blooms all around the stem, not just on one side. *D. grandiflora* and *D. lutea* have yellow blooms.

Epimedium species and cultivars
epimedium (barrenwort)
4"–12" tall
Pink, yellow, violet, crimson, white blooms
Flowers spring
Light shade
Zones 4–8
Use as a groundcover

Heart-shape foliage, often evergreen, is veined red as it emerges in spring. Hardly ever needs dividing. Very easy to grow. Spurred flowers are bicolored except in white and yellow cultivars.

Doronicum caucasium
leopard's bane
18"–24" tall
Yellow blooms
Flowers early spring
Sun to partial shade
Zones 3–8
Use in border and woodland gardens

Prefers humusy, well-drained soil. Handsome heart- to kidney-shape leaves near ground level; daisy-like flowers rise above them. Ephemeral perennial that disappears in hot weather. Good companion for spring bulbs.

Eupatorium maculatum
joe-pye weed
6'–10' tall
Rosy purple, wine-red blooms
Flowers late summer
Sun to light shade
Zones 3–8
Use in border, butterfly, cutting, and
    naturalistic gardens

North American native. Very easy to grow. Suitable for back of a border. Combine with ornamental grasses, asters, and goldenrod. 'Atropurpureum' has purple-tinted foliage.

Euphorbia polychroma (E. epithymoides)
cushion spurge

8"–10" tall
Chartreuse and bright yellow blooms
Flowers spring
Sun to light shade
Zones 6–11
Use in border, container, and Xeriscape
gardens, and as a groundcover

Clump-forming; leaves, sometimes tinged
purple, turn deep red in fall. Clusters of tiny
flowers. Undemanding, self-sows freely. Myrtle
spurge (*E. myrsinites*) is hardy from zones 5 to 8.

Filipendula rubra
queen–of–the–prairie

5'–9' tall
Slightly fragrant, pink, deep rose blooms
Flowers early to midsummer
Light shade
Zones 3–9
Use in border, naturalistic, and butterfly
    gardens

North American native. Prefers moist, rich soil.
Striking at the rear of a border with its large,
deep green, divided leaves and fluffy plumes.
Doesn't need staking. Combines well with
Japanese iris. 'Venusta' has deep rose flowers.

Galium odoratum
sweet woodruff

6"–8" tall
White blooms; fragrant foliage
Flowers late spring to early summer
Light shade
Zones 4–8
Use as a groundcover

Scent of stems, especially when dried, is
reminiscent of new-mown hay. In centuries
past, sweet woodruff was strewn on the floor
to scent a room. Combines well with other
shade-loving perennials, such as hostas and
ferns. Prefers moist soil.

perennial plants

Geranium species and cultivars
cranesbill

4"–24" tall
Blue, pink, purple, rose, red, white blooms
Flowers late spring to summer or fall
Sun to light shade
Zones 5–9
Use in border, container, rock, and
    naturalistic gardens and as groundcover

Lovely at the front of a border. Avoid
afternoon sun in hot zones. Excellent cultivars
include 'Johnson's Blue', 'Wargrave Pink', and
'Striatum'. Combines well with dianthus, hosta,
blue oat grass, and other ornamental grasses.

Gypsophila paniculata
baby's breath

2'–3' tall
White, pink blooms
Flowers summer
Sun
Zones 3–8
Use in border and cutting gardens

Creates a delicate, airy filler in the garden.
Combines well with roses, cranesbill, lavender,
and salvias. 'Bristol Fairy' has double white
blooms; 'Pink Fairy' is smaller, growing to
1½ to 2 feet tall, with double pink flowers. Cut
back after first flush of bloom for a second
flowering. May need staking. Flowers can be
used fresh or dried in arrangements.

Hedera species and cultivars
ivy

20'–50' tall
No flowers
Sun to shade
Zones 4–9
Use as a vine for containers, as a groundcover,
    or in a cutting garden

English ivy (*H. helix*) is best known. Aggressive
and invasive; it can disguise a fence in 2 to
3 years. Cultivars include 'Glacier', with foliage
splotched white, slower-growing 'Needlepoint'
with very small leaves. Plants that die back
to the ground in winter may revive from the
roots in spring. Prune to control spread.

Helianthemum species and cultivars
rock rose (sun rose)
9"–18" tall
Yellow, apricot, crimson, pink blooms
Flowers early summer
Sun
Zones 5–9
Use in border, rock, and Xeriscape gardens
   and as groundcover

Sprawling plant with gray-green leaves.
Provide protective mulch in cold-winter areas.
Easy care but may be short-lived. Cut back
after bloom for second flowering in fall.
'Raspberry Ripples' is a good cultivar.

Hemerocallis species and cultivars
daylily
1'–3' tall
All colors (no blue); bicolor blooms, some fragrant
Flowers early to late summer;
Sun to light shade
Zones 4–9
Use in border, butterfly, and cutting gardens
   and as a groundcover

One of the easiest to grow (and most hybridized)
of all perennials. Usually each flower lasts only a
day. Tolerates drought when not in bloom. Some
are evergreen in warm zones. Look for tetraploids.

Heliopsis helianthoides
false sunflower
30"–60" tall
Yellow, gold blooms
Flowers summer to fall
Sun
Zones 4–9
Use in border, cutting, naturalistic, and
   Xeriscape gardens

Native to North America. Brightly colored,
daisylike flowers. Does not need staking. Single
or double blooms. 'Loraine Sunshine' has
white leaves variegated with green
veins. Combines well with asters, Shasta
daisy, garden phlox, and speedwell.

Heuchera sanguinea
coralbells
18"–24" tall
Pink, white, rose, red blooms
Flowers late spring to late summer
Sun to light shade
Zones 3–9
Use in border, butterfly, cutting, and rock
   gardens, and as a groundcover

Native to North America. Grown as much for
its evergreen foliage as its flowers. Ruffled
leaves often purple-bronze ('Palace Purple'),
marbled silver ('Frosty'), or variegated cream.
For rebloom, cut off spent flower stems. Long-
lived. Provide winter mulch in northern zones.

Helleborus species and cultivars
hellebore
12"–18" tall
Green, white, cream, mauve, rose, pink blooms
Flowers late winter to early spring
Light shade
Zones 5–8
Use in border, cutting, and naturalistic
   gardens, and as a groundcover

Color when virtually nothing else is in bloom:
H. niger, Christmas rose, flowers January to
March; *H. orientalis*, Lenten rose, blooms March
to mid-May. Many hybrids between the two.
Dislikes heat and transplanting.

Hibiscus moscheutos
rose mallow (swamp rose mallow)
3'–4' tall
Light and deep pink, rose, white blooms
Flowers late spring to summer
Sun to light shade
Zones 5–9
Use in border, container, and cutting gardens

Native to southern North America. Huge
blooms are striking in the garden. Prefers
moist, well-drained soil. Excellent cultivars
include magenta pink 'Ann Arundel',
'White Giant', and crimson 'Southern Belle'.

Hosta species and cultivars
hosta
6"–36" tall
Lavender, blue, white blooms, some fragrant
Flowers summer
Partial sun to shade
Zones 3–9
Use in border, containers, and as groundcover

Excellent foliage plant for shade gardens. Slender, lance-shape, heart-shape, or rounded leaves in chartreuse, green, or blue, often variegated or edged in white or gold. May be bothered by slugs or black vine weevils.

Iberis sempervirens
candytuft
9"–12" tall
White blooms
Flowers spring
Sun
Zones 4–8
Use in border and rock gardens

Evergreen foliage attractive year-round. Easy to grow, not troubled by pests or diseases. Shear after flowering to keep plants compact. Combines well with spring-flowering bulbs. There are many cultivars. 'Autumn Beauty' and 'Autumn Snow' rebloom in fall.

Jasione laevis (J. perennis)
sheep's bit
5"–18" tall
Blue blooms
Flowers summer
Sun to light shade
Zones 5–9
Use in border, cutting, and rock gardens

Same family as bellflowers. Not often grown but makes a lovely border edging. Produces flowers, which resemble those of scabiosa, throughout summer. Prefers sandy soil. 'Blue Light' has vivid blue flowers on 2-foot stems.

perennial plants

Kalimeris pinnatifida
kalimeris
2'–3' tall
White blooms
Flowers summer to fall
Sun
Zones 5–9
Use in border, butterfly, and cutting gardens

Formerly known as *Boltonia cantoniensis*, kalimeris combines well with boltonia as well as asters, goldenrod, chrysanthemums, and ornamental grasses. Doesn't need staking. The species has white blooms, which help soften dramatic color contrasts.

Kirengeshoma palmata
yellowbells
3'–4' tall
Pale yellow blooms
Flowers late summer to early fall
Partial sun to light shade
Zones 5–9
Use in border and naturalistic gardens

Graceful plant that resembles a shrub with its deciduous, maple-shape leaves on reddish purple stems. Makes an excellent specimen plant in moist but well-drained soil.

Knautia macedonica
knautia
18"–24" tall
Wine red blooms
Flowers summer to fall
Sun
Zones 5–9
Use in border, cutting, and naturalistic gardens

Tall, slender, lax stems weave among other perennials and ornamental grasses. Self-sows freely but not invasively; seedlings are easy to pull up in spring and transplant or discard. Prefers well-drained soil.

Kniphofia species and cultivars
red hot poker (torchlily)
18"–60" tall
Flame red, orange, cream, pink, yellow blooms
Flowers summer to fall
Sun
Zones 6–10
Use in border, container, cutting, and
   naturalistic gardens

Stunning plant for the border. A tender
perennial in cold zones; mulch well or dig up
and store roots for winter. Scores of cultivars.

Liatris spicata
gayfeather (blazing star)
2'–3' tall
Reddish purple, white, blue, violet blooms
Flowers summer to fall
Sun to light shade
Zones 3–10
Use in border, butterfly, cutting, and
   naturalistic gardens

Native to North America. Flowers open from
the top down. Easy to grow; no pests or
diseases. Prefers moist, well-drained soil. Cut
flowers are long-lasting, as is the plant itself.

Lamium species and cultivars
lamium (dead nettle)
12"–18" tall
Pink, white, purple, yellow blooms
Flowers late spring to summer
Light shade to full shade
Zones 3–10
Use in border and container gardens, and as a
   groundcover

Can be invasive; easy to grow; tolerant of dry
shade. Shear after flowering; foliage has all-
season appeal, often variegated or brushed with
silver or pale green. 'Beacon Silver' has silver
leaves edged in green, pink blooms; grows to 8
inches. 'Pink Pewter' (shown) is deeper pink.

Ligularia species and cultivars
leopard plant
24"–30" tall
Fragrant bright orange, yellow blooms
Flowers mid- to late summer
Partial sun to light shade
Zones 4–9
Use in border, container, and naturalistic
   gardens

Wonderful for its serrated, round, or arrow-
pointed foliage all season; leaves of some
cultivars are purple ('Desdemona', 'Othello').
L. stenocephala 'The Rocket' reaches 4 feet in
height. Needs constantly moist soil to flourish.
Mulch for winter protection in cold zones.

Leucanthemum vulgare
ox-eye daisy (marguerite)
15"–36" tall
White blooms with yellow centers
Flowers late spring to early summer
Sun to light shade
Zones 5–9
Use in border, butterfly, and cutting gardens

Easy to grow in constantly moist but well-
drained soil. Deadhead for continuous bloom.
Related to Shasta daisy, which has many
cultivars with single, semidouble, and double
flowers, including 'Snowcap' and 'Agalia'.

Lilium species and cultivars
lily
2'–7' tall
Fragrant white, pink, red, maroon, yellow,
   orange, and bicolor blooms
Flowers early to late summer
Sun
Zones 4–8
Use in border, container, and cutting gardens

From Asiatic hybrids flowering in June to
Oriental hybrids in August and species in
between and beyond, there is a lily for every
garden. Many species are native to North
America. Easy to grow; requires good
drainage; tall cultivars may need staking.

117

Liriope species and cultivars
lilyturf
12"–15" tall
Dark mauve, lilac, white blooms
Flowers late summer to early fall
Sun
Zones 6–10
Use in border, cutting, and naturalistic gardens

Evergreen, arching, grasslike foliage. Cut back old foliage in early spring. Leaves may be variegated white or yellow. Cultivars include yellow-striped 'Variegata', large-flowered 'Monroe White', and rich violet 'Majestic'.

Lobelia cardinalis
cardinal flower
2'–4' tall
Scarlet, white, pink blooms
Flowers mid to late summer
Sun to light shade
Zones 2–9
Use in border, butterfly, hummingbird, and naturalistic gardens

Native to North America. Usually short-lived but self-sows freely. Prefers constantly moist soil. 'Alba' has white blooms; 'Rosea', pink.

Lupinus Russell Hybrids
lupine
3'–4' tall
Pink, red, blue, yellow, white, bicolor blooms
Flowers late spring to summer
Sun to light shade
Zones 4–7
Use in border, cutting, butterfly, and naturalistic gardens

Prefers cool, evenly moist, acid soil. Challenging to grow and worth it when it blooms en masse in midborder. Reseeds. Cut off spent flower stalks to promote rebloom. Attractive foliage. Combines well with Siberian iris and salvias.

perennial plants

Lychnis coronaria
rose campion
1'–2' tall
Cerise blooms
Flowers early summer
Full to partial sun
Zones 3–9
Use in border, container, naturalistic, and cutting gardens, and as a groundcover

Grayish white, hairy leaves; stems bear small, solitary flowers. Short-lived but reseeds freely. Easy to grow in any soil; will survive in parts of Zone 9 where humidity is not high. 'Alba' has white flowers; 'Ocellata', white with a bright pink eye; 'Flore Pleno' is double-flowered.

Lysimachia punctata
yellow loosestrife
2'–3' tall
Bright yellow blooms
Flowers early to late summer
Sun to light shade
Zones 4–9
Use in border, butterfly, and naturalistic gardens, and as a groundcover

Tall with upright whorls of yellow blooms. Old-fashioned, easy to grow. Can spread invasively. Gooseneck loosestrife (*Lysimachia clethroides*) grows about 2½ feet tall with nodding racemes of white blooms.

Monarda species and cultivars
beebalm
2'–3' tall
Scarlet, white, pink blooms; fragrant leaves
Flowers summer
Sun
Zones 4–8
Use in border, butterfly, and hummingbird gardens

Native to North America. Intriguing flower form. Frequented by hummingbirds and butterflies. Susceptible to powdery mildew; 'Violet Queen' is more resistant than some others. Dwarf form, 'Petite Delight', grows to only 15 inches tall.

Nepeta x *faassenii*
catmint
18"–24" tall
Fragrant pale lavender, white blooms
Flowers summer
Sun to light shade
Zones 3–9
Use in border, butterfly, and container gardens,
    and as a groundcover

Soft, silver-gray leaves. Spreads readily. 'Six
Hills Giant' has deeper violet flowers;
'Snowflake' has white blooms. Flowers are
sterile; propagate by division. Cats love it!

Opuntia species
prickly pear (cholla)
6"–96" tall
Yellow, orange, red, pink, purple blooms
Flowers late spring to early summer
Sun
Zones 3–11
Use in border, container, and Xeriscape gardens

Native to North America. The hardiest include
plains prickly pear, *O. polyacantha* (to Zone 3);
hardy prickly pear, *O. compressa (humifusa)*, to
Zone 4; and walking-stick cactus, *O. imbricata*
(to Zone 6). Need well-drained soil. Combines
well with grasses, succulents, and conifers.

Oenothera fruticosa
sundrops
18"–24" tall
Bright yellow blooms
Flowers early summer
Sun
Zones 4–9
Use in border and naturalistic gardens,
    and as a groundcover

Native to North America. Blooms during
the day, unlike fragrant evening primrose
(*O. macrocarpa [missouriensis]*). Attractive red-
tinged, evergreen leaf rosettes. Spreads quickly;
control by pulling up unwanted plants.

Paeonia lactiflora cultivars
peony
18"–36" tall
Fragrant pink, white, red, and bicolor blooms
Flowers late spring to early summer
Full to partial sun
Zones 3–8
Use in border and cutting gardens

Single, anemone, semidouble, and double-
flowered forms. Early, midseason, and late-
blooming cultivars. Foliage makes attractive
backdrop for later-blooming perennials. Very
long-lived. Support plant with wire hoops.
Cut stems to ground in fall; discard. Scores of
cultivars; select by color and season of bloom.

Omphaloides cappadocica
omphaloides (navelwort)
6"–9" tall
Blue–and–white blooms
Flowers mid- to late spring
Light shade to shade
Zones 5–8
Use in naturalistic gardens and as a groundcover

Related to forget-me-nots. Sprays of bicolored
flowers are lovely against the dark green
foliage. Spreads slowly to about 18 inches.
Prefers moist, well-drained soil. Easy to grow.

Paeonia suffruticosa cultivars
tree peony
3'–6' tall
Fragrant white, carmine, purple, yellow, pink
    blooms
Flowers late spring
Sun
Zones 6–8
Use in border gardens and as a specimen

Long-lived. Needs rich, moist, well-drained
soil. Plant where it has shelter from harsh
winds; protect from rabbits the first year with
wire cage. Large flowers; remove them as soon
as they fade to deter botrytis fungus.

Papaver orientale cultivars
oriental poppy

3'–4' tall
Pink, salmon, raspberry, red, white blooms,
    often splotched black-purple at base
Flowers late spring to early summer
Sun
Zones 3–8
Use in border, container, and cutting gardens

One of the showiest flowers for the border.
Easy care; will grow in almost any well-
drained soil. Leaves disappear by midsummer.

Pediocactus simpsonii var. *minor*
hedgehog cactus

2"–8" tall
Pink, magenta, white, yellow blooms
Flowers late spring to summer
Sun
Zones 6–11
Use in border, container, and Xeriscape gardens

Native to North America. Most are difficult to
grow on their own roots. This species is easy
to raise from seed, cuttings, or a graft. Grows
2½ inches tall, may form clumps, survives
cold winters best with a covering of snow.

Penstemon species and cultivars
beard-tongue (penstemon)

2'–4' tall
Red, pink, lavender, blue, white blooms
Flowers early to late summer
Sun
Zones 3–10, depending on species
Use in border, hummingbird, naturalistic, and
    Xeriscape gardens

Native to North America. Short-lived; finicky
about adapting outside its natural environment.
Needs excellent drainage. Susceptible to crown
rot; mulch with gravel, not organic material.
Most reseed freely.

perennial plants

Perovskia atriplicifolia
russian sage

3'–5' tall
Lavender, blue blooms; aromatic foliage
Flowers late summer to fall
Sun
Zones 5–9
Use in border and butterfly gardens

Silvery gray hairs cover the stems and
lanceolate or dissected leaves. Might get floppy
late in the season but remains attractive. Easy
to grow in well-drained soil. Provide winter
mulch in cold zones; cut back hard in spring.
Basically pest- and disease-free.

Phlox divaricata
wild sweet william

8"–12" tall
Blue, white blooms; slightly fragrant
Flowers midspring
Partial sun to light shade
Zones 3–9
Use in border and naturalistic gardens, and as
    a groundcover

Spreads slowly; never invasive. 'Fuller's White'
has white blooms; var. *laphamii* has deep
purple-blue flowers. Combines well with
bleeding heart and naturalized spring-
flowering bulbs. Evergreen in the South.
Prefers well-drained soil.

Phlox paniculata cultivars
garden phlox (summer phlox)

2'–4' tall
Fragrant pink, lavender, white, red blooms,
    often with deeper colored eye
Flowers mid- to late summer
Sun to light shade
Zones 4–9
Use in border, butterfly, and cutting gardens

Backbone of the perennial garden. Prefers rich,
well-drained soil; heavy feeder. Cut off spent
blooms for continuous flowering. Prone to
powdery mildew; do not water overhead. Select
resistant cultivars: lavender-blue 'Chattahoochee',
lavender 'Katherine', and white 'David'.

Phlox subulata
moss phlox (mountain pink)
4"–6" tall
Pink, white, blue, lavender, red blooms
Flowers midspring
Sun
Zones 2–9
Use in border and rock gardens, and as a
    groundcover

Foliage is semievergreen in the North, evergreen
in the South. Combines well with spring-
flowering bulbs. Prefers sandy, well-drained
soil. Shear after flowering. 'Red Wings', 'White
Delight', and 'Blue Hills' are good cultivars.

Polygonatum species and cultivars
solomon's seal
1'–3' tall
Greenish white blooms
Flowers late spring
Light shade
Zones 4–8
Use in naturalistic and woodland gardens

Native to North America. Easy care; needs
moist soil. Related European *P. odoratum*
'Variegatum' has fragrant flowers, which attract
hummingbirds, and cream-edged leaves.

Platycodon grandiflorus
balloon flower
18"–36" tall
Blue, white, pink blooms
Flowers early summer to fall
Sun to light shade
Zones 3–8
Use in border and cutting gardens

Intriguing, puffy buds like little balloons open
to star-shape blooms, which keep appearing if
you cut off spent blooms. Needs staking.
Long-lived perennial. Slow to break dormancy
in spring, so mark where you plant it.
Cultivars: white 'Albus', Shell Pink', 'Mariesii'.

Primula species and cultivars
primrose
6"–18" tall
Pink, white, blue, crimson, and bicolor blooms
Flowers early spring to early summer
Partial sun to light shade
Zones 5–9
Use in border, container, rock, and
    naturalistic gardens, and as a groundcover

Charming plants to light up shady spots.
Scores of cultivars, colors, and forms from
simple clusters to candelabra types. Needs
moist, acidic soil. Very pest-prone.

Polemonium caeruleum
jacob's ladder (greek valerian)
1'–2' tall
Blue blooms
Flowers late spring
Light shade to sun
Zones 3–9
Use in border and naturalistic gardens

Prefers moist, well-drained soil. Foliage,
arranged in rung-like fashion along the stems,
adds texture to the border or woodland.
Susceptible to mildew. There are white 'Album'
and variegated cultivars.

Pulmonaria species and cultivars
pulmonaria (lungwort)
8"–12" tall
Deep rose, coral red, blue, white blooms
Flowers spring
Light to full shade
Zones 3–9
Use in border and naturalistic gardens, and as
    a groundcover

Spreads quickly in moist soil. Easy to grow;
slugs may be a problem. Foliage is attractive all
season. *P. officinalis, P. longifolia,* and *P. saccharata*
have white-spotted leaves. Many cultivars.

Ranunculus acris
meadow buttercup
12"–15" tall
Bright yellow blooms
Flowers late spring to summer
Sun
Zones 5–8
Use in naturalistic gardens and as a groundcover

Easy to grow in any well-drained soil; reseeds with abandon. A favorite of children. 'Flore Pleno' is a double-flowered form, *Ranunculus repens* 'Buttered Popcorn' has finely dissected foliage edged in silvery green (zones 4–9).

Ratibida columnifera
prairie coneflower (mexican hat)
1'–2' tall
Yellow, brownish red blooms
Flowers summer
Sun
Zones 3-9
Use in border, bird, butterfly, cutting, and naturalistic gardens

Native to North America. Short-lived but reseeds. Not fussy but needs well-drained soil. Very finely dissected leaves. Combines well with ornamental grasses.

Rudbeckia species and cultivars
black–eyed susan
2'–3' tall
Yellow, bronze blooms
Flowers midsummer to fall
Sun
Zones 3-9
Use in border, butterfly, cutting, and naturalistic gardens

Native to North America. Easy to grow; long-lasting flowers; not fussy about soil or moisture. Not long-lived; reseeds prolifically. *R fulgida* blooms in July; 'Goldsturm' is a reliable 2-foot-tall cultivar. Combines with most perennials.

perennial plants

Salvia species and cultivars
salvia (sage)
1'–5' tall
Fragrant pink, white, lavender, blue, red blooms
Flowers early to late summer
Full sun to light shade
Zones 4-9
Use in border, butterfly, container, cutting, edible, naturalistic, and Xeriscape gardens

Sage for cooking; salvias for ornamentation. Attractive green, grayish, or variegated foliage and spikes of flowers. Undemanding and easy to grow. Many are native to North America. Some, such as culinary sage, are woody; cut back in spring before new growth begins.

Santolina chamaecyparissus
lavender cotton
18"–26" tall
Yellow blooms; fragrant foliage
Flowers early summer
Sun
Zones 6-10
Use in border and Xeriscape gardens

Grow this plant for its gray, divided foliage, not for the flowers. Makes an attractive low, clipped hedge around beds. Needs well-drained soil. Protect with a winter mulch in cool zones. Cut back plants in spring. 'Lambrook Silver' has silver foliage; 'Plumosus' has very lacy, silver foliage. *S. rosmarinifolia* is a green-leaved species.

Saponaria ocymoides (S. officinalis)
soapwort (bouncing bet)
4"–8" tall
Pink, red, white blooms
Flowers summer
Sun
Zones 3-8
Use in border and rock gardens

Mat-forming. Flower clusters practically cover the foliage; shear after flowering to keep it compact. Easy to grow in any soil. Cultivars include the tiny 'Bressingham', which grows to only 1 inch tall, and 'Rosea', with rose-colored flowers. Attractive along a path.

Saxifraga species and cultivars
saxifrage
3"–6" tall
Pink, carmine, white, yellow blooms; some fragrant
Flowers early to late summer
Light shade
Zones 3–8
Use in border and rock gardens, and as a groundcover

Clump-forming. Many have grayish green leaves; leaves of *S. stolonifera* (strawberry geranium) are white-veined above, red below. Likes moist soil; dislikes hot summers.

Solidago species and cultivars
goldenrod
1'–3' tall
Yellow blooms
Flowers late summer to fall
Sun to light shade
Zones 3–10
Use in border, butterfly, cutting, and native gardens

Native to North America. Cultivars are more garden-worthy and less invasive than species: 'Crown of Rays', 'Goldenmosa', dwarf 'Golden Thumb'. Easy to grow in average soil.

Sedum species and cultivars
sedum
6"–24" tall
Pink, red, white, yellow, orange blooms
Flowers late spring to fall
Sun
Zones 3–9
Use in border, butterfly, container, Xeriscape, and rock gardens, and as a groundcover

Foliage is attractive all season. Clump-forming or creeping. Easy to grow. Deep red seedpods follow yellow blooms on *S. kamtschaticum*. The trailing stems of *S. spurium* 'Dragon's Blood' root where they touch soil. Pink flowers of *S. spectabile* (now *Hylotelephium*) 'Autumn Joy' and 'Vera Jameson' deepen to rusty rose by fall.

Stachys byzantina
lamb's ears
12"–18" tall
Pinkish purple, mauve, magenta blooms
Flowers late spring to summer
Sun
Zones 5–8
Use in border gardens

Grown for its silvery, velvety foliage; the cultivar 'Silver Carpet' does not produce flowers. Easy to grow except in hot, humid climates. *S. officinalis* (betony) has green, crinkled foliage and reddish purple flower spikes. Reseeds freely.

Sidalcea malviflora
checkerbloom
(miniature hollyhock)
2'–4' tall
Pink, white, red, purple blooms
Flowers mid- to late summer
Sun to light shade
Zones 5–9
Use in border, container, and cutting gardens

Native to North America. Easy to grow. Needs well-drained soil. Seldom needs staking. Cut back after first flowering to promote rebloom. 'Elsie Heugh' has fringed, light pink blooms; 'Scarlet Beauty' has deep purple flowers.

Stokesia laevis
stokes' aster
1'–2' tall
Blue, white, pink, and pale yellow blooms
Flowers late summer
Sun to light shade
Zones 5–10
Use in border, butterfly, and Xeriscape gardens

Native to North America. Evergreen in the South. Long-flowering and easy to grow almost anywhere. Needs well-drained soil. Withstands heat and drought. Protect with mulch in winter in cold zones.

123

Tanacetum parthenium
feverfew
12"–30" tall
White blooms with yellow centers
Flowers summer
Sun to light shade
Zones 5–9
Use in border, cutting, and naturalistic gardens

Easy to grow but not reliably hardy; self-seeds freely. Cut back after first flowering for rebloom in late summer. Foliage is aromatic. There are double- and yellow-flowered and yellow-leaved ('Aureum') forms.

Thalictrum species and cultivars
meadow rue
3'–5' tall
Pink, purple, lavender, yellow, and white blooms
Flowers early to late summer
Sun to light shade
Zones 5–8
Use in border, container, and naturalistic gardens

Graceful plant for rear of border or woodland planting. Blue-green leaves resemble those of columbine. Easy to grow, long-lived; prefers moist, well-drained soil. Flowers have sepals and prominent stamens, no petals. *T. flavum* ssp. *glaucum* is the most heat tolerant (Zone 9).

Thermopsis villosa
carolina lupine
3'–5' tall
Yellow blooms
Flowers early to midsummer
Sun to light shade
Zones 3–9
Use in border and naturalistic gardens

Native to North America. Attractive, divided foliage all season. Long-lived. Good specimen or rear-border plant. Combines well with ornamental grasses, wildflowers. May need staking if grown in rich soil or light shade.

perennial plants

Thymus species and cultivars
thyme
1"–12" tall
Fragrant lilac, crimson, pink, white blooms
Flowers in early summer
Sun
Zones 5–9
Use in border, container, edible, and rock gardens, and as a groundcover

So many to choose from; all easy to grow. Keep soil on dry side; cut back in spring. Gray-green or variegated leaves. Creeping thyme, *Thymus serpyllum*; lemon-scented, *T. × citriodorus*; silver, *T. vulgaris* 'Argenteus'; woolly, *T. pseudolanuginosus* (blooms insignificant).

Tiarella cordifolia
foamflower
6"–12" tall
White, pink, rose, maroon blooms
Flowers late spring
Sun to light shade
Zones 3–8
Use in border and woodland gardens, and as a groundcover

North American native. Pair with early spring bulbs, columbines, and ferns. Dislikes hot, dry climates; likes moist, acidic soil. 'Major', salmon pink blooms; 'Marmorata', purple-flecked leaves, maroon flowers; 'Purpurea', bronze-purple foliage, rose flowers. Spreads by underground runners.

Tradescantia virginiana
spiderwort
18"–30" tall
Blue, red, purple, magenta, pink, white blooms
Flowers late spring to summer
Sun to light shade
Zones 4–9
Use in border, container, and naturalistic gardens

Long-lived perennial. Easy to grow; not fussy about soil. Reseeds prolifically. Might rebloom in fall if entire plant is cut back when leaves begin to yellow. There are many cultivars, including 'Zwanenburg Blue', with intensely blue flowers; 'Rubra', deep rosy pink; 'Snowcap', white; and 'Congesta', purple.

Tricyrtis species and cultivars
toad lily
1'–3' tall
White, lilac, purple-spotted blooms
Flowers fall
Light shade to shade
Zones 5–9
Use in border and woodland gardens

Unusual plant with orchidlike blooms. Lovely by a path; combines well with hellebores, hostas, and ferns. Needs moist, slightly acidic soil. *T. formosana* 'Amethystina' has clusters of amethyst blue flowers; *T. hirta* 'Miyazaki', white blooms spotted lilac along arching stems.

Verbena species and cultivars
vervain
6"–48" tall
Purple, pink, and white blooms
Flowers summer to early fall
Sun
Zones 3–10
Use in border, container, and Xeriscape gardens

Very tolerant of drought and heat. Often reseeds freely. Rose verbena, *V. canadensis*, is often grown as an annual. Blue vervain, *V. hastata*, is long-blooming. *V. rigida* 'Alba' has white flowers. *V. bonariensis* is hardy to Zone 7.

Trillium species and cultivars
wake–robin (trillium)
1'–1½' tall
Pink, white, maroon, and yellow blooms
Flowers mid- to late spring
Light shade
Zones 3–8
Use in naturalistic and woodland gardens

Native to North America. Never collect from the wild; buy plants only from nurseries that can confirm that the plants are nursery-propagated (not just nursery-grown). Grows best where there is winter snowcover and on the West Coast. Prefers moist, well-drained soil. Combines well with bleeding hearts, primroses, epimedium, and ferns.

Veronica species and cultivars
speedwell (veronica)
1'–2' tall
Fragrant pink, rose, white, blue blooms
Flowers summer
Sun
Zones 4–8
Use in border and container gardens

Easy to grow. If soil is too rich, stems may sprawl and need staking. Cut back spent flowering stems to promote rebloom. Popular cultivars include pink 'Minuet', deep violet-blue 'Sunny Border Blue', true blue 'Crater Lake Blue', and 'White Icicle'.

Verbascum species and cultivars
mullein
2'–3' tall
Pale to sunny yellow blooms
Flowers early to late summer
Sun
Zones 4–8
Use in border and naturalistic gardens

Many mulleins are biennial, which produce large flower spikes in the second year. The perennials are not long-lived but do reseed. Needs well-drained soil. There are also white, pink, and purple species and hybrids.

Vinca minor
periwinkle (creeping myrtle)
2"–12" tall
Blue, white blooms
Flowers midspring
Sun to shade
Zones 4–9
Use as a groundcover

Evergreen. Spreads rapidly but not invasively by rooting along the stems. Easy to grow. Combines well with spring bulbs. 'Alba' has white flowers; 'Ralph Shugert', white-edged leaves; 'Flore Pleno', double-flowered blue.

shade-garden stars

Whether you look for a groundcover, a delicate backdrop for spring-blooming perennials and bulbs, or an easy-care filler, consider ferns. Although ferns are usually associated with shady, woodland areas where they are indispensable, many ferns will also grow well in gardens that receive dappled sunlight or a small amount of direct sun in the early morning or late afternoon, but not at midday (too hot and burning).

design considerations

Combine with broad-leaved plants, such as hellebores, hostas, and wild ginger, to accentuate the delicate appearance of feathery ferns. Taller ferns, such as ostrich and cinnamon, look good interplanted with evergreen shrubs.

Tall or short ferns combine well with spring-flowering bulbs. The fronds will camouflage the dying, yellowing foliage of the bulbs. Ferns add a lovely airy aspect to a garden. They are ideal fillers, as well.

cultural factors

The majority of ferns prefer moist, rich soil, but a few will grow on drier ground. Do not plant them too deep: Set the crowns at or just below ground level and cover with thin layer of soil. Mulch the area well to keep mud off the fronds and to conserve soil moisture.

While a fern is getting established in your garden, keep the soil constantly moist. If you plant ferns in sun or in warm zones, provide extra water through the growing season.

Adiantum pedatum
maidenhair fern
Deciduous
1'–2' tall
Shade to partial sun
Zones 3–8
Use in border, container, and naturalistic
   gardens, and as a groundcover

This is a tough, hardy plant, despite its delicate appearance, with pale green fronds on wiry stems. The fronds of southern maidenhair, *Adiantum capillus-veneris* (hardy only to Zone 8), emerge bronze-pink in spring and turn pale green as they mature. Needs constantly moist, lime-enriched soil.

Athyrium nipponicum 'Pictum'
japanese painted fern
Deciduous
12"–18" tall
Light shade to shade
Zones 3–8
Use in border and woodland gardens, and as
   a groundcover

Tricolored fronds make this one of the most beautiful ferns. Old fronds make a good mulch, so don't bother to remove them. Needs constantly moist, well-drained soil. Combines well with purple-leaved plants, such as 'Palace Purple' coralbells, and blue-leaved hostas.

fabulous ferns

Cyrtomium falcatum
holly fern
Evergreen
2'–3' tall
Partial sun to shade
Zones 6–10
Use in container and woodland gardens

Plants (native to Hawaii) grow well in containers, which you can bring indoors for winter in cold zones. Leaflets resemble leaves of English holly. Do not bury the crown when you plant. Site it in a sheltered spot. The related *Cyrtomium fortunei* (also called holly fern) is also hardy to Zone 6; it needs very well-drained soil to forestall rot in winter.

Dennstaedtia punctilobula
hay-scented fern
Deciduous
24"–30" tall
Shade to sun
Zones 3–9
Use in naturalistic gardens, and as a
   groundcover

Fronds smell like new-mown hay when crushed. Easy to grow, it tolerates wet or dry soil, sun or shade. Spreads fast; not recommended for small gardens. Excellent as a groundcover on a slope.

Dryopteris cristata
crested wood fern

Semievergreen
12"–30" tall
Light shade to shade
Zones 4–8
Use in border and woodland gardens

Fertile fronds stand erect and are taller than the sterile fronds. Prefers wet soil but will adapt to regular garden conditions if the soil is kept very moist. *D. clintoniana*, which may be a hybrid of *D. cristata* and *D. goldiana* (Goldie's wood fern), has broader, taller fronds.

Osmunda cinnamomea
cinnamon fern

Deciduous
2'–5' tall
Light shade to shade
Zones 3–8
Use in woodland gardens, and as a
    groundcover

Can be invasive but easy to pull up as it emerges in spring; spreads by underground runners. Fertile fronds are erect and dark brown. Sterile fronds form a shuttlecocklike rosette. Adaptable to sunny sites if provided with ample moisture.

Matteuccia struthiopteris
ostrich fern

Deciduous
3'–5' tall
Shade to sun
Zones 3–8
Use in woodland and naturalistic gardens,
    and as a groundcover; edible

Small, fertile fronds turn cinnamon brown as they mature. Loves wet, swampy soil but will grow in drier areas. Very hardy plant and easy to grow. Spreads slowly. You can collect the new spring fronds (the fiddleheads) to eat boiled or raw in salads.

Polystichum acrostichoides
christmas fern

Evergreen
18"–24" tall
Shade to partial sun
Zones 3–8
Use in cutting and woodland gardens, and as
    a groundcover

Native to North America. Fiddleheads are silvery haired as they emerge. Adaptable and easy to grow. Can tolerate more sun than most ferns, provided it has sufficient moisture. Appropriately named, it is long-lasting when cut for use indoors.

You can remove dead fronds in late fall, although they will decompose on their own, adding humus to the soil. In cold-winter climates, mulch the planting area as protection against the alternate freezing and thawing of the ground.

other attractive ferns

In addition to the ferns shown here, you may want to consider these:

lady fern, *Athyrium filix-femina*, has finely divided fronds. It is delicate in appearance but not in reality. Tolerant of sun, it makes an excellent groundcover in constantly moist soils in zones 3–8.

japanese sword fern, *Dryopteris erythrosora*, is evergreen. Its fronds are rosy brown when they emerge; they become rich green as they mature. It is hardy to Zone 5 (to Zone 4 with a winter mulch for protection).

sword fern, *Nephrolepis exaltata*, is a familiar houseplant and also an outdoor groundcover in shade or partial sun in mild climates (zones 9–11). Its large, 5-foot fronds are evergreen.

soft shield fern, *Polystichum setiferum*, has narrow fronds that lie close to the ground. Like lady fern, it appears delicate, but it is quite hardy and is tolerant of dry, poor soils. Hardy to Zone 5.

tassel fern, *Polystichum polyblepharum*, is evergreen with stiff fronds. It needs light to full shade and constant moisture. It grows in a vase shape to about 2 feet. Hardy in Zones 4–9.

cultivating beauties

Ornamental grasses prefer well-drained soil. With a few exceptions, they are drought- and heat-tolerant.

To take advantage of the extended seasons of interest of ornamental grasses, wait until spring to cut back leaves and flower stalks. The fluffy plumes remain attractive through winter, and the seeds often provide food for birds. Tall ornamental grasses look beautiful planted where early morning or late afternoon sun will shine through the foliage and plumes.

Note that many grasses that are tame garden subjects in colder zones can become aggressively invasive in mild climates, such as those of California and Florida.

Cortaderia selloana
pampas grass
6'–9' tall
Silver-white leaves, plumes tinged red or purple
Flowers midsummer to early winter
Sun to light shade
Zones 7–10
Use in cutting gardens, and as a specimen plant

A stately, architectural plant. The razor-sharp leaves are evergreen in mild climates. Prefers moist soil. 'Gold Band' has yellow-edged leaves. Compact, dwarf 'Pumila' grows 4 to 6 feet tall, appropriate for a border. It can be invasive.

Calamagrostis acutiflora 'Stricta'
feather reed grass
6'–7' tall
Green tinged reddish bronze to buff plumes
Flowers early summer
Sun to partial sun
Zones 5–9
Use in border and cutting gardens; as a specimen

Very showy, cool-climate grass. Tolerates wet or dry conditions and poor soil. Seed heads ripen from gold to silver through summer and fall. 'Karl Foerster' is shorter, 5 to 6 feet, and blooms slightly earlier.

Festuca glauca
blue fescue
6"–18" tall
Blue-green foliage
Flowers summer
Sun
Zones 4–9
Use in border, container, and rock gardens

Lovely, tufted plant with steel blue leaves that last well into winter. Remove flowers, if you want, to concentrate attention on the foliage. Prefers dry, well-drained soil. Suffers in hot summer weather but recovers when temperatures cool. 'Elijah Blue' grows to 8 inches, with soft blue foliage; 'Glauca Minima' has intensely blue leaves.

ornamental grasses

Carex stricta 'Bowles Golden'
bowles golden sedge
2' tall
Creamy silver plumes
Flowers late spring
Sun to light shade
Zones 5–9
Use in border gardens, and as a specimen plant

Sedges (there are more than 1,000 species and cultivars) are grasslike perennials. Most often grown near or in water; must be constantly wet to thrive. Most will grow in light shade, where they combine well with ferns and hostas.

Hakonechloa macra
hakone grass
1'–1½' tall
Reddish pink plumes
Flowers late summer to fall
Partial sun to light shade
Zones 5–9
Use in border and container gardens, and as a groundcover

Green, weeping foliage, reminiscent of bamboo; turns pinkish red in fall. Spreads slowly. Brightens shade gardens. 'Aureola' (shown) produces yellow leaves striped with narrow green lines; foliage burns in full sun, less yellow in deep shade.

Helictotrichon sempervirens
blue oat grass
1½'-2' tall
Straw-colored marked purple plumes
Flowers late spring to summer
Sun to partial sun
Zones 5–9
Use in border, container, and rock gardens

Rigid, steel blue or blue-green foliage. Attractive, small grass; like blue fescue but larger. Evergreen in warm climates. Does not like heavy, clay soils. Combines well with blue-leaved shrubs or contrasting perennials.

Panicum virgatum
switch grass
6'–7' tall
Pink, red, silver plumes
Flowers summer to fall
Sun to light shade
Zones 5–9
Use in cutting and naturalistic gardens, and as a specimen

North American tallgrass prairie native. Tolerates range of soils, climates, and moisture. Leaves turn yellow in fall. Forms tight, vertical clumps. 'Heavy Metal has pale metallic blue leaves.

Imperata cylindrica 'Red Baron' ('Rubra')
japanese blood grass
12"–18" tall
None
Sun to light shade
Zones 5–10
Use in border and container gardens, and as a specimen

This variety is grown for bright, wine red foliage, which becomes scarlet by fall. Effective when backlit by the setting sun. If a plant reverts to all-green, remove it immediately. (The green-leaved species spreads aggressively. A noxious weed, it cannot be sold in this country.

Pennisetum alopecuroides
fountain grass
3'–4' tall
Pink, white, and rose plumes
Flowers summer
Sun to light shade
Zones 6–9
Use in border, container, and cutting gardens

One of the most popular grasses for the middle and rear of a border. Plumes on laxly arching stems. Easy to grow; somewhat drought-tolerant. Dwarf 'Hameln' grows 1½ to 2 feet tall; does not grow well south of Zone 8. Very dwarf 'Little Bunny', only 12 inches tall, is a good rock-garden plant.

Miscanthus sinsensis 'Zebrinus'
zebra grass
5'–6' tall
Silver, tan plumes
Flowers summer
Sun
Zones 6–9
Use in border and bird gardens, and as a specimen

Very popular and easy to grow. Will grow near or in ponds. Leaves of 'Zebrinus' and 'Strictus' (porcupine grass) have horizontal bands of yellow. 'Gracillimus' has showy flowers. 'Purpurascens' has orange-red fall color.

Pleioblastus species
bamboo
18"–72" tall
No flowers; grown for handsome leaves
Sun to light shade
Zones 6–9
Use in Oriental-style gardens, and as a specimen and screen plant

Stems (culms) are hollow. Peaceful rustling when it moves in a breeze. Contain bamboo with concrete edging at least 2 feet deep if it is a running, not clumping, species. Pygmy bamboo, *P. pygmaeus*, and dwarf white–striped bamboo, *P. variegatus*, are good garden choices.

designing with rainbow plants

Iris are aptly named for the goddess of the rainbow. They have flowers in every hue, including a wide range of blues. You will want them in your garden, though, for more reasons than that: They are easy to grow, bloom from early spring to summer (depending on the varieties you choose), and are just as beautiful in a vase indoors as they are in the garden. They are, however, much longer lasting in the garden.

Although there are some iris that reflower in fall, most do not rebloom. Their leaves, however, are attractive vertical accents for months. Plant iris in a border with almost any other perennial that has similar or contrasting growth habits: daylilies, peonies, dianthus, columbines, ferns, cranesbills, hostas, and primroses. Hostas are particularly effective with iris that have variegated leaves.

a bit of definition

Falls: The outer, usually drooping row of petal-like sepals, often a darker color than the rest of the flower.

Standards: The inner row of petals, which may lie horizontally across the falls or stand upright.

Beard: A fuzzy tuft emerging from the blossom throat and continuing down the falls. It is usually a different color, often yellow, than the petals.

Signal: Markings of contrasting color at the base of the falls; they attract insects, such as bees, and show them the way in to the pollen. Veins along the petals and beards provide the same guidance.

Self: A flower with falls and standards of the same color.

Iris cristata
crested iris
6"–12" tall
Lavender-blue, purple, white blooms
Flowers midspring
Sun to light shade
Zones 6–9
Use in border, container and naturalistic gardens, and as a groundcover

Native to North America. The earliest iris to bloom. Exquisite plant. Spreads slowly. Provide extra water in sunny gardens. 'Alba' has white flowers.

iris

Iris × germanica
bearded iris (german iris)
18" tall
Fragrant deep and pale violet blooms
Flowers late spring
Sun
Zones 3–10
Use in border and cutting gardens

One of the parents of modern bearded iris. Its origin is unknown; it might actually be a natural hybrid. The flowers are quite large. Easy to grow. Tolerant of many soil and climate conditions. *I. × germanica* var. *florentina* has very pale blue standards.

Iris ensata (kaempferi) cultivars
japanese iris
2'–3' tall
Fragrant violet, blue, lavender, yellow, white blooms
Flowers early summer
Sun to light shade
Zones 6–9
Use in border, cutting, and water gardens

One of the last iris to bloom. Attractive near or in ponds and streams. Intolerant of limey soils. Scores of hybrids, many of which are tetraploids (extra chromosomes), which produce larger, longer-lasting flowers.

Iris hybrids
louisiana iris
2'–4' tall
Blue, pink, red, purple, yellow blooms
Flowers late spring to summer
Sun to light shade
Zones 4–9
Use in border and cutting gardens

Louisiana hybrids include several species native to southern North America and their natural and man-made hybrids. The beardless flowers are lovely. Plants are adaptable but prefer moist soil while in bloom. Tolerate heat and humidity; some go dormant in summer.

Iris pallida
orris (dalmation iris)
3'–4' tall
Fragrant lilac–blue, lavender blooms
Flowers late spring to early summer
Sun
Zones 4–9
Use in border gardens

The root is used as a fixative in perfumery and potpourri. A parent of the modern tall bearded iris. The silvery green leaves may be semievergreen. There are varieties with striped leaves: 'Variegata' (cream), 'Alba Variegata' (white), and 'Aurea Variegata' (yellow).

Iris sibirica
siberian iris
2'–3' tall
Blue, purple, magenta, pink, white, yellow
   blooms
Flowers late spring to early summer
Sun to light shade
Zones 3–9
Use in border and cutting gardens

Beardless. Grasslike leaves are attractive all summer. Easy to grow. Graceful flowers with hybrids in a wide range of colors and bicolors: white and yellow 'Butter and Sugar', red–purple 'Ruffled Velvet', deep blue self 'Swank'.

Iris pseudacorus
yellow flag
2½'–5' tall
Yellow, white blooms
Flowers early to midsummer
Sun to light shade
Zones 3–9
Use in border, cutting, and water gardens

A beardless iris at home near or in water. Reseeds freely. Adapts to garden conditions as long as you provide constant moisture. 'Alba' has creamy white blooms. The leaves of 'Variegata' start out yellow-striped and mature to green.

Iris versicolor
blue flag
2'–3' tall
Blue blooms, blotched yellow with purple veins
Flowers late spring to early summer
Sun to light shade
Zones 3–9
Use in border, cutting, and water gardens

Native to eastern North America. Prefers wet conditions; will adapt to garden conditions if constant moisture and humus-rich soil are provided. The rhizome is highly poisonous. Southern blue flag, *I. virginica*, grows to 2 feet.

cultural factors
Most iris prefer moist to wet soil and, especially in warm zones, some protection (shade) from midday sun. Plant bearded iris with the rhizome at the soil surface.

The best time to dig up and divide most iris is in fall. Most are so adaptable, however, that you can divide them anytime they are not in bloom, although midsummer would certainly reduce their chances for survival.

Remove yellowed, dead foliage in late fall and compost or discard it.

other beautiful iris
dwarf iris, *Iris verna*, has very fragrant, violet-blue flowers from mid- to late spring. Beardless, it is native to eastern North America. The foliage is evergreen in mild climates. Hardy in zones 6–9.

red iris, *I. fulva*, is a lovely native plant with rusty red flowers that are more open and flat-topped than other iris. It blooms in late spring and needs very moist soil. Hardy in zones 6–9.

gladwin iris, *I. foetidissima*, is also known as stinking iris, an appropriate name because the foliage is malodorous. The seeds are the reason for its inclusion in so many gardens. The seedpods open in autumn to reveal unusual and decorative, reddish orange seeds that persist through winter. The leaves are evergreen. Hardy in zones 5–9.

winter iris, *I. unguicularis*, starts to bloom in December in areas with very mild winters and continues through February. It has fragrant, violet-blue flowers, which are good for cutting, and evergreen foliage. Hardy in zones 8–10.

131

color overview

color your world

Color is a matter of perception. The colors you see exist as a result of an eye-brain connection. What truly exists as pure light, human experience tints with meaning. The colors you see have a powerful capacity to paint a rainbow of emotions. This proves especially true in a garden.

No object actually possesses color. A polar bear's fur coat is composed of transparent fibers that reflect light, making them appear white. The ocean is clear water seen as blue because of its depth and how it shines in the sunlight. A rose looks red or yellow to you, but what a bee senses are the radiant markings that will bring it close to the flower's nectar.

Full-color vision probably evolved to help humans identify food and predators, and ultimately to survive. Now it has become the tool for much more leisurely and enjoyable pursuits, such as gardening.

Sir Isaac Newton first explored how humans perceive color. Refracting sunlight through a simple pinprick on paper, he discovered a band, or spectrum, of colors representing unabsorbed light. Newton invented the color wheel to show arrangements within this spectrum. Leonardo da Vinci later developed color theory as a way to explain the contrasting and complementary kinships among colors that he observed in nature.

vibrant monochrome
above right: **Cannas, zinnias, amaranth, and cosmos stand up and sing in a chorus of red within a pocket garden.**

landscape painting
right: **A palette dominated by pinks, gray-greens, and lavenders and anchored with rounded gray boulders and a gazebo colors this gentle landscape.**

Human ability to understand and enjoy color has evolved through time. Early humans were conscious only of primary colors, seeing the world in bloody reds, heavenly blues, and sunny yellows. Those first colors of human experience still have an instinctive pull, but modern life stimulates people by offering more complex palettes in everything from house paint and appliances to flowers.

Like a prism, your own garden reflects the beauty of the world seen through the light of your experience. The colors you choose will translate that vision.

fiery corner

left: **The warm tones of a climbing rose, a redwood arbor, and yellow foxgloves transform a dark corner into an exciting, flowery destination. Glimmering white chairs and the flair of blue accents add finishing touches.**

color overview

the garden canvas

When you break ground for a garden, you'll dab your plant paintbrush into both universal and personal responses to color. That language gives you tools to create moods. Energetic oranges and reds, which urge motion and stimulate appetite, fit well along paths and around dining areas. Serene blues and greens induce tranquillity. In a meditation garden or other seating area, they paint the scene with a sense of peace. Like a baroque concerto, pinks and lavenders soothe with harmonious notes. Purples and deep reds introduce mysterious chords. White, seen in a flattering light, offers refuge and cool refreshment.

The palette of plant choices constantly expands as breeders develop new plant varieties. Although new flower and foliage colors don't keep the fast pace of fashion color trends, certain colors enjoy peaks of popularity. Orange flowers and golden, red, and variegated foliage represent current favorites.

flower fashions

above: **This window box wears the hottest trends in annual flowers, including 'Peaches 'n' Cream' verbena, diascia, million bells (*Calibrachoa* spp.), orange abutilon, and zonal geranium.**

color whimsy

above: Color blooms among the furnishings
of this outdoor dining room. Cheerful
hues of yellow, blue, and green combine
in a cozy setting brimming with smaller,
decorative elements.

pastel fantasy

left: Tranquil color choices of blue and white
create a restful nook inside a front gate.
The white arbor, wrought-iron furnishings,
and salvaged door add dreamlike, timeless
elements. The fountain and drifts of white
flowers make this garden a twilight destination.

color overview

play of light

The landscape's colors may appear dazzling, subdued, or nearly invisible by turns, reacting to the sun's intensity. Every corner of your garden canvas shines when you learn how to play with light: which colors appear radiant at twilight, which look brightest at high noon, and which shine like candles in shade. A true "color gardener" knows how to juggle colors in balance with given light conditions and other natural surroundings.

Terms such as saturation, shade, tone, and tint explain why colors appear bright, dark, similar, or light. As you become familiar with seasonal changes and how the sun moves across your landscape, you'll gain visual skill at staging different colors in the light, deciding when a saturated versus a tinted color, or a pastel versus a bright, best fits in your garden's constantly changing choreography of color and light.

blue moods

right: The skillful use of color extends into every level and aspect of this blue-theme garden, from the latticed arbor to the fence to the knob-head alliums and blue-gray agaves in lead urns.

summer harmonies

below: A border of bright perennials, including Asiatic lilies, lythrum, and monkshood, synchronize their blooming rhythm to the summer sun.

color your garden

How can you work with your chosen colors, blend them with a contrasting or transitional hue, and segue those brushstrokes into a garden masterpiece? Study the relationships among colors. Gather leaves and flowers from your favorite plants and play with them in a vase or on a sheet of plain paper, juxtaposing textures and hues until you find a balance that pleases your eye. Some garden designers also recommend collecting paint chips in your intended palette and using them to color-match at the garden center as you search out furniture and ornaments.

Use this book to lay the groundwork for your garden. First, explore the qualities and effects of each color and learn which blooms and leaves contain them. Find out which colors work best together, which linking colors to use, and how to contrast or subdue plant colors. Build color relationships that flow throughout the garden.

Discover which plants deliver the most enduring color in the garden. You'll also learn how to sustain colorful plantings throughout the growing season and year-round, as well as how to multiply them to get the most from your color budget. Spend the bulk on trees and shrubs that will provide colorful highlights in more than one season. Get lots of filler color inexpensively by growing annuals from seed.

Travel through the pages to the gardens of five artists who share tips on working with color. Following their footsteps, consider furnishings and accessories to complete your own garden's colorful statement. Then try a project or two and give it your own unique spin. Now take up your garden paintbrush and begin. Your adventures with color start here!

portrait in pinks
left: **A vignette of soft pink perennials, such as lythrum, *Lavatera* 'Barnsley', and fragrant phlox, refreshes a midsummer setting.**

ultimate yard *&* garden | **137**

colors & their companions

pink 140
red 144
orange 148
yellow 152
green 156
blue 160
purple 164
lavender 168
white 172
silver 176
rainbow 180

pink

From spring's first trilliums and cherry blossoms to the last wave of starry asters in a fall border, pink is a crowd pleaser among flower colors. Always fresh faced and calming, it links islands of deeper, more intense colors with soothing tones. Pink serves as an instant, visual pick-me-up that's reassuring and cheerful. Many of the garden pinks you know have softly sentimental echoes: Old Garden roses, hollyhocks, sweet peas, and foxgloves stand out among nostalgically favorite pink flowers.

think pink

- Plant pink flowers around concrete statuary and birdbaths to soften the harsh grayness of the concrete.
- Blossoms of trees and shrubs paint the garden in seasonal spring or summer pink. Redbud, dogwood, weigela, clethra, cherry, crabapple, beautybush, and butterfly bush bear pink blooms.
- Pinks, or dianthus, came by their name not for their rosy coloring but for the flowers' serrated, or pinked, edges.
- Light up the shade with pink-flowering perennials, including astrantia, epimedium, foxglove, bleeding heart, and cyclamen.
- Look no farther than your feet for pink-flowered groundcovers: poppy mallow, creeping thyme, sedum, and heather.

Clockwise, from opposite top:
Rosa × hybrida
'Carefree Beauty' rose
This single-petal Griffith Buck rose blooms all summer and endures winter extremes as cold as Zone 4. It traces its heritage to antique pink garden roses.

Rhododendron spp., Clematis spp.
'Antoon van Welie' rhododendron,
'Nelly Moser' clematis
Hardy evergreen rhododendrons and azaleas contribute vibrant pinks in spring. The clematis hybrid blooms in late spring and often again in late summer.

Aster novae-angliae
New England aster
A native North American wildflower improved through breeding, this plant is a stalwart of late summer and fall.

Paeonia spp.
peony
Winter chilling prompts this hardy perennial's brief but fragrant spring flowers. Plant the growing points, or eyes, no more than 2 inches deep to ensure blooms.

Digitalis purpurea, Rosa spp.
foxglove, unidentified rose
Their light-dark contrasts of pinks make these plants a picture-perfect duo.

pink

The many faces of pink range from the barely-there blush that tints spring crabapple blossoms to the throbbing magenta found in dianthus, portulaca, and hibiscus. If a delicate pink flower in your border deserves more attention, plant it next to white. White spotlights even the palest hues.

Look also on the lighter side of the pink spectrum for effective linking colors. Puddles of light pink enrich adjacent deep blues, golden yellows, and deep cerise pink. The one richly saturated color that doesn't benefit from pink is red. A side-by-side contrast of the two colors ends up looking flat. But if the pink has a peachy cast with tints of yellow, then adjacent red flowers will pop visually.

Use silver foliage as a partner for pink to separate more intense hues in a long flower border. One of pink's most effective harmonies occurs with blues of all shades. Pale hues of pink and blue merge in mauve. Find it in varieties of monkshood, delphinium, hellebore, and lilac. Mauve looks muddy unless woven skillfully into the garden. Deep, saturated pinks, violets, and dark blue help clarify and define mauve; silver sidekicks set off its satiny sheen.

Pink invariably hits it off visually with green. A green, white, and pink planting trio provides instant refreshment. Looking for a good match for hot pink? Try equally jazzy versions of green: lime green or yellow-green. Think magenta zinnias paired with bells of Ireland.

Clockwise, from opposite top:

Astilbe spp., *Dianthus barbatus* astilbe, sweet William
The 15-inch-tall border pink, or sweet William, comes in vivid shades of magenta and carmine, a beautiful foil to feathery, peachy pink astilbe.

Rosa spp.
'Bonica' Shrub rose
A frothy, pale pink and white border of Shrub roses and perennials romances a split-rail fence at the height of summer.

Rosa spp., *Iris spuria*
'Belinda's Dream' rose, spuria iris
These tall, hardy irises spread in hospitable climates. Their slender yellow blooms synchronize with the first flowering of the Shrub rose in early summer.

Paeonia, Phlox divaricata peony, woodland phlox
Both of these fragrant perennials flower in late spring or early summer. Plant them in light shade as a bulb cover.

Lilium hybrid
Asiatic lilies
A pink and yellow lily duet freshens up the border in midsummer along with shiny pink lavatera. Plant lilies in fall or early spring.

red

Red tantalizes our impulsive side. It excites and energizes, stirring us with the primal color of fire, sunsets, and blood. Red varies from vermilion and scarlet to crimson and maroon. Its association with passion and prosperity across the globe also gives red cultural significance. Like a flamenco dancer strutting across the stage, red commands attention. Unpredictable and volatile, red inspires risk taking. Need a visual bull's-eye in the border? Opt for red flowers or foliage as the exclamation marks in your garden palette.

Clockwise, from opposite top:
Zinnia elegans
zinnia
Annual flowers such as these introduce quick bursts of vibrant red into the summer landscape.

Papaver somniferum
breadseed poppy
Scatter annual poppy seed in lawns, meadows, and flower borders wherever a splash of summer red will stand out.

Dianthus deltoides
maiden pink
This fragrant member of the carnation family features bunches of serrated flowers that attract butterflies. It's a short-lived perennial that's hardy to Zone 3.

Crocosmia masoniorum
'Lucifer' crocosmia
Crocosmia's wands of fiery flowers sprout from bulbs. Plant after the danger of frost passes; lift and store indoors before the ground freezes in cold climates.

Zinnia elegans, Canna × hybrida
zinnia, canna
When pairing these two tender plants, use taller zinnia varieties on the same eye level as the canna flowers. Lift canna tubers and store them inside in cold-winter areas.

seeing red

- Jarring on a large scale, red tends to dominate a scene. Use it sparingly for best results.
- In thin, weak spring light, red brightens the entire garden. Summer morning and evening light kindles a glow in red petals that appears harsh in midday sun. In fall, red looks deeper and richer; it has a warming effect.
- Red flowers (especially tubular-shape ones) signal hummingbirds that nectar awaits.
- Botanical (Latin) plant names often allude to their color. *Cardinalis, coccineus, rosea, rubra, ruber,* and *sanguineus* all refer to kinds of red.
- Weave red accents, such as linens and candles, into your outdoor living areas for a cheery how-do-you-do when company calls.

red

Red takes on different properties depending on what colors you pair with it. The most effective framing color for a red-flowered standout is its complement: green. When a border focuses on green foliage, a single red-flower or red-leaf accent truly shines.

Include red in your garden's color scheme by partnering it with silver or white. Silver calms red into good behavior in a border; white offers a crisp contrast to richly colored reds

Write mystery into your garden plots by combining the deep reds, such as burgundy, maroon, and russet, with equally dark purple and chocolate brown. Such sultry combinations create the illusion of depth and hidden distances.

Red berries, twigs, and bark create magic in the winter garden against a snowy background.

Clockwise, from opposite top:

Tulipa spp., *Muscari* spp.
tulip, grape hyacinth
A red and blue medley delivers strong color to early-spring gardens. Plant masses of these hardy bulbs in late fall.

Lobelia spp.,
Perovskia hybrid
lobelia, Russian sage
Featuring the same spiky silhouette, these two perennials pair in a striking combo.

Sedum 'Autumn Joy',
Aster × *frikartii 'Monch'*,
stonecrop,
Frikart's aster
Lavender and red-orange warm the fall garden with perennial color. The asters' golden centers echo the fuzzy texture of the sedum blooms.

Knautia macedonica,
Anethum graveolens
pincushion, dill
The burgundy perennial and the yellow annual feature similar wiry stems.

Salvia farinacea,
S. splendens
mealycup sage,
scarlet sage
Many of summer's richest hues come from the blue and red blooms of annual salvias.

orange

Orange mixes the cheerfulness of yellow and the boldness of red into an attention-grabbing burst of volcanic energy. Hot orange's tropical nature and its universal popularity, especially in Latin cultures, has made it a sought-after garden and fashion color. Orange appeals for its sunlit radiance and for the way it piques our appetite. The color, which includes pumpkins, peaches, and citrus in its culinary repertoire, also attracts hummingbirds and butterflies when it appears in flowers.

let orange shine

- Orange holds its own in sunny, bright exposures. Choose hot orange flowers for hot climates and softer peaches and apricots for regions that frequently experience cool, cloudy weather.
- Because orange enhances appetite and promotes sociability, plant plenty of orange-flowering plants near outdoor eating areas.
- Incorporate orange into your garden by using brick walls and paths, terra-cotta pots and statuary, and copper trellises and birdbaths.
- Include plants that bear orange fruits: pyracantha, sea buckthorn, and bittersweet, as well as some roses and hollies.

Clockwise, from opposite top:

Papaver nudicaule
Iceland poppy

A perennial, often biennial, this cold-climate poppy unfurls rich-hue, silken flowers atop 2- to 3-foot-tall stems during late spring's cool weather.

Cosmos sulphureus
'Klondike' cosmos

Easily grown from seed, this dwarf annual offers waves of brilliant orange throughout the summer.

Lilium hybrid
Asiatic lily

This intense orange bloomer harmonizes with white, pink, pale orange, or blue summer flowers.

Asclepias tuberosa
butterfly weed (milkweed)

Flower clusters on these lanky plants open in mid- to late summer and attract droves of butterflies.

Kniphofia
red hot poker

Brush-shape, tubular flowers characterize this heat-hardy perennial. The varied combinations of red, orange, and yellow flowers attract hummingbirds.

orange

Bring out the best in both bold and pale oranges by blending them with their color wheel complement: blue. When you contrast fiery orange flowers with blue and yellow ones, the border sizzles. Deep blue *Salvia farinacea* combined with orange-yellow calendula or peachy verbascum results in a magnificent effect. You'll get comparably classic results from a trio of orange, red, and blue.

Purple also marries with orange in a sophisticated color composition. Both contain red values, ensuring compatibility. Sometimes the colors crop up on the same plant, as in the magnificent multitints of *Euphorbia griffithii* 'Fireglow'. On the blue side of purple, lilacs and lavenders also flatter deep orange.

Mingle orange flowers with pink and you end up with a plant painting that's

slightly dissonant but delicious. Add white or pale yellow to knit the two other colors together. Similarly, cream and bronze partners moderate orange. Orange and white duos create vignettes with a fresh feel. If the white flowers have orange or yellow centers, the match works even better.

Combining orange with lime green brings out the yellow values in both colors. This duet works wonderfully in the shade when the orange blooms of trollius, azalea, or tiger lily stand out among chartreuse foliage. Complete this sensational shady scenario by adding purple-leaf plants.

Pale orange hues, such as peach, salmon, and apricot, harmonize happily with silver-leaf plants, especially in cloudy climates. Imagine peach-color roses skirted with artemisia, rue, or lavender. 'Southern Charms' verbascum or 'Brompton Apricot' stock combine peach-color petals and silvery foliage all in one.

Clockwise, from opposite top:
Lilium hybrid, *Silene* spp.
Asiatic lily, catchfly
This early-summer scenario entails planting drifts of lilac around the feet of lilies. An annual native to America, silene self-seeds freely.

Cosmos sulphureus, Salvia guaranitica
cosmos, salvia
This complementary pair thrives in the summer heat. The salvia survives mild winters only; otherwise, it's best grown as an annual.

Eschscholzia spp., *Leucanthemum* × *superbum*
California poppy, Shasta daisy
Sow poppy seeds on hillsides, in vacant lots, or in country gardens and celebrate summer as their gleaming petals unfurl. Shasta daisy spreads in undisturbed areas too.

Abutilon hybrid, *Ageratum houstonianum*
flowering maple, 'Blue Horizon' flossflower
The tall, billowy blossom annual grows to just the right height to mingle with abutilon, a tender tropical that can move indoors over winter.

Calendula officinalis, Antirrhinum hybrid
pot marigold, snapdragon
Enjoy the flower power as these annuals keep up their show throughout summer and fall.

yellow

Yellow delivers an invitation to smile. It never fails to cheer. As the color closest to that of the sun, it's only fitting that yellow announces the spring with a deluge of daffodils and forsythias, and then rules over the summer garden with unflagging brightness. It closes the fall as the last golden leaf twirls to the ground. Yellow emanates a sense of well-being that's instantly, and joyously, absorbed. If smiles and hopes had a color, it would be called yellow.

Clockwise, from opposite top:

Helianthus annuus
annual sunflower

Sunflowers epitomize the summer season. Include 3-foot-tall dwarf varieties, such as 'Teddy Bear' and 'Sunspot', in your summer yellow paintbox for excellent cut flowers.

Lysimachia punctata
yellow loosestrife (circleflower)

This heirloom, prized by pioneer Americans, thrives in partial sun and moist soil. The 3-foot-tall golden-flowering perennial can become invasive.

Thunbergia alata
black-eyed Susan vine

Grown from seed, this tropical annual drapes a hanging basket, window box, or trellis for the summer. It fares best in a sunny spot with regular watering.

Hemerocallis hybrid, *Heliopsis helianthoides*
'Hyperion' daylily, 'Golden Feathers'
false sunflower

This monochromatic planting of bright and pale yellows pairs perennials timed to bloom in early summer. Gain more plants by digging and splitting mature plants every third spring.

Acer palmatum
Japanese maple

These colorful, slow-growing small trees thrive in moist soil and shade. Plant them under oaks with azaleas and ferns for a woodland effect.

harness the power of yellow

- Yellow increases a sense of space. A narrow side yard or dim courtyard takes on a bright new look when it features plantings with a yellow theme.
- Yellow appears fresh and radiant on the hottest days. Use yellow flowers and leaves in window boxes and baskets to create a warm, cheerful look.
- Pale yellows illuminate night gardens. Welcome the moonshine potential of such flowers as 'Moonbeam' coreopsis, evening primrose, *Brugmansia,* santolina, 'Anthea' or 'Moonshine' yarrow, and 'Lady Banks' rose.
- Fill in with green-and-yellow variegated foliage to showcase neighboring flowers of purple, bright pink, or red.

ultimate yard *&* garden | 153

yellow

Although we normally think of yellow as an intense color that can overpower, use paler shades to link other, brighter colors effectively. Pale creamy yellow has a calming influence on other flower colors. Combine it with pale pink, blue, or white, especially in cool, overcast climates where more gaudy shades of yellow appear jarring. An all-yellow planting combining different shades looks cheerful yet sophisticated.

Yellow radiates in the shade where it pairs beautifully with pale greens, lime green, or green–yellow or green–white variegated foliage. Strong yellows for shady places include Japanese maple, kerria, ligularia, lysimachia, azalea, and rhododendron.

Increased plant choices in yellow-foliage varieties also now exist. The glow of golden-leaf shrubs, such as barberry or euonymous, among the greens turns up the wattage in a foliage garden. Here,

yellow leaves provide the visual interest that flowers usually supply.

When bright yellow joins up with orange and its complement, blue, it sets an energetic harmony into motion. Yellow enhances both colors. When it contains a hint of orange, yellow becomes a showstopping dance partner with bright or light blue. The blue slightly mutes yellow's boldness and brings out its luminescence.

The same effect happens with yellow's opposites on the color wheel: purple and dark red. They look even better when seen in the company of yellow. Generously sprinkle yellows, both pale and bright, in areas exposed to early- or late-day sunlight, when yellow reflects rather than absorbs light.

Clockwise, from opposite top:

Hydrangea macrophylla, Rudbeckia hirta, Lilium hybrid
bigleaf hydrangea (mophead), black-eyed Susan, Asiatic lily
This trio brightens a cloudy-climate garden. Plant the medley of shrub, perennial, and bulb in spring and enjoy the way it warms the gray concrete accent for summers to come.

Allium spp., Lilium hybrid
flowering onion, Asiatic lily
Flowering bulbs in complementary colors make a sensational duo for early-summer gardens. The lily acts as a natural stake for the slender allium stalk.

Solidago spp., Echinacea spp.
goldenrod, purple coneflower
Partnered with another native prairie perennial, goldenrod fills the border with flowers that echo the color of late-summer sunshine.

Rosa hybrid, Myosotis scorpioides
'Graham Thomas' rose, forget-me-not
Delicate sprays of perennial forget-me-nots fill in the gaps among English roses. Bright blue and apricot flowers invariably make a stunning combination.

ultimate yard & garden | **155**

green

Green frames the jewel-like beauty of flowers so well that you might take its shady reassurance and new-leaf innocence for granted. Most garden color flows from nature's cornucopia of greens, from mosses and groundcovers to leafy shrubs and trees. Sophisticated garden designs often rely on green's infinite variety. Sunlight plays out a daily drama, transmuting vital greens to liquid golds or forest-dark, deep mysteries by turns.

Clockwise, from opposite top:

Lysimachia congestiflora
variegated creeping Jenny

A collage of variegated gold-and-green lysimachia, along with chartreuse hosta leaves and two varieties of fern, provides a perennial tapestry in the shade.

Iris sibirica, Matteuccia struthiopteris
Siberian iris, ostrich fern

Two perennials for rich, moist soil unfurl their new green finery and flowers in late spring.

Petroselinum spp.
parsley

As the first color of spring in the kitchen garden, a contrast of flat- and curly-leaf biennial parsley creates a textural study in green. Mulching plants lightly in fall helps them survive winter.

Hebe cupressoides, Juniperus spp.
hebe, juniper

Rugged evergreen groundcovers, including hebes and junipers, join creeping thymes to show off various tints of green combined with flattering hues of bronze and gold.

Acer palmatum
Japanese maple

An excellent understory tree, the Japanese maple's leaves unfold like graceful fans.

the planting o' the green

- Choose green arbors, benches, fencing, furniture, and containers whenever possible. They'll enhance nearby flower colors.
- Contrast different shades of green foliage in deep shade, where some of the showiest flowering plants won't thrive. Use chartreuse, yellow, and variegated green-white or yellow-green foliage plants for the most pronounced effects. Add light-color statuary, a birdbath, a bench, or a temporary pot of vibrant flowers to make this area of your garden shine.
- Green flowers offer novel appeal. Try viburnum, lady's mantle, tulip, hellebore, bells of Ireland, and hydrangea. These make great cut flowers too.
- Many plants lend their names to shades of green, including pea, olive, fern, bean, lime, kiwi, mint, and ivy. It's no wonder there's a green named spring!

ultimate yard *&* garden | **157**

green

The green season begins with the pale green cones of uncurling hostas and coils of fiddlehead ferns. Summer deepens new green into mature shades. Boulders, tree trunks, and ponds may disclose the startling lime green of lichens, mosses, and algae. Mediterranean and other dry-climate plants offer a palette of dusty gray-greens that diffuse the sun's burning rays through summer's hottest days.

Green makes shady places appear fresh and cool, especially when the picture is woven with white flowers or variegated foliage. Two-tone leaves that pair green with white, silver, or gold dapple the shade with bright highlights. In coleus, houttuynia, and tovara leaves, green mingles with reds, purples, and blues, resulting in a wide palette of possibilities for shade.

Consider nearby greens when placing intense flower colors in the border. Green tinged with red ensures an effective union between deep, dramatic red and purple or yellow and purple. Chartreuse or yellow-green foliage brings out the best in purple and yellow combos. The blue-green of hosta and yucca leaves flatters pastels and (in generous portions) makes small spaces appear larger.

Clockwise, from opposite top:

Sedum spurium
creeping sedum

Fine-textured perennial creeping sedum thrives in a cracked concrete birdbath that no longer holds water.

Juniperus horizontalis 'Wiltonii'
horizontal blue juniper

Among a colorful cast of shrub characters, including Harry Lauder's walking stick, blue spruce, chartreuse false cypress, and 'Mugo' pine, groundcover juniper sprawls at center stage.

Hydrangea spp., Hosta hybrid
hydrangea, hosta

Layers and shades of green dotted with white and orange glow in this shady oasis that also includes lilies, impatiens, and coral bells.

Pelargonium spp., Impatiens hybrid
'Peppermint Star' geranium, impatiens

The textures of two annuals form a dynamic contrast. Chartreuse geranium foliage frames and clarifies red impatiens blossoms.

Pinus spp., Acaena spp., Imperata cylindrica
pine, bidi–bidi, Japanese blood grass

Not a flower in sight, yet this interplay of textures from an ornamental grass, a perennial groundcover, and an evergreen renders an always fresh and intriguing composition.

blue

Blue offers peaceful depths for our contemplation.

Heavenly blue has a spiritual side that evokes serenity and inspires wonder. Promising limitless horizons in water, sky, and garden borders, it invites the beholder to wade in and get lost. Cool, calming blue anchors hotter, more emotional colors in pools of natural tranquillity. Blue fascinates as it dances with light. Spring's pale light brings out the silvery side of blue. In the heat of summer, blue appears clear and bright—refreshing as a mountain lake.

get the garden blues

- Clear blues emerge in spring forget-me-nots and columbines; campanulas give way to irises in early summer. As high summer approaches, bold blues take over with aconite, baptisia, clematis, and delphinium.

- Add blue to your landscape in the form of ornamental fruits: blueberry, porcelain berry, bayberry, and juniper.

- In hot, dry climates, blue appears as strong and limitless as the sky. In damp regions, blue and green merge. In shade and at dusk, blues seem violet, whereas violet seems pink, so place cool-color plants in areas where they'll shine true.

Clockwise, from opposite top:

Muscari spp.
grape hyacinth
Plant the tiny bulbs in fall and enjoy the exceptional spring display of blooms. Place masses of bulbs under fruit trees, along edges of beds, or in a rock garden.

Salvia uliginosa
bog sage
This brilliant blue-flower perennial thrives in damp soil with a sunny exposure. Grow it as an annual for fall color in cold-climate areas.

Convolvulus spp.
morning glory
The intensely sky blue flower saucers on this annual vine have made it an all-time favorite for generations of gardeners.

Delphinium elatum
delphinium hybrids
Delphiniums require a bit of pampering to produce their regal, perennial flower spikes. Stake each plant to support the flowers throughout their summer show.

Hydrangea macrophylla
mophead hydrangea
Unsurpassable for summer color in the shade, hydrangea shrubs produce flower clusters in shades of pink, blue, or white, depending on the variety and the soil pH.

blue

Blue's recessive quality serves as a beautiful blender for other colors and makes it appear warm or cool relative to its tint and plant companions. Cool, pale blue flowers, especially those that appear in spring, knit other colors together. For subtle, impressionistic contrasts, combine blue with its cool cousins: lavender, gray, and green.

Blue, in any hue, mingles well with pink, yellow, and its opposite: orange. Borders painted with blue, yellow, and orange or a trio of blue, red, and lime green, add pizzazz to summer landscapes. Blue has a stabilizing effect when placed near electric colors such as chartreuse, magenta, crimson, or hot pink.

The frosty blues of fall that tint ornamental kale and Russian sage interact dramatically with other autumnal colors, including deep oranges, reds, and violets.

As intermediary colors in the garden, blue and silver work well together, creating restful scenes where eyes can take refuge. The two colors merge in the foliage of plants such as rue, juniper, blue fescue, *Rosa glauca*, and *Hosta sieboldiana*. Blue-flower plants with silvery foliage, including lupine, baptisia, pulmonaria, mertensia, and many salvias, have a double impact on the landscape. Like silver, white clarifies blue's ambiguity. Blue and white combinations bond easily, creating a crisp, polished look.

It's that visual ambiguity that makes blue the perfect vehicle for conjuring illusions of depth. Placed at a border's end, or in the background, it creates an impression that the space goes on and on. If you want to connect your garden's boundaries and the surrounding landscape, blue provides a gentle blending tool. Establish a contemplative area around a fountain or garden bench by using tranquil blue flowers and foliage.

Clockwise, from opposite top:
Nepeta spp., *Salvia* spp., *Artemisia* spp.
catmint, salvia, artemisia
A restful planting focuses on this flower-bearing statue, surrounding it with a sea of blue and gray textures from hardy perennials.

Antirrhinum hybrid, *Salvia farinacea*
snapdragon, mealycup sage
These annuals work well as a combo because of their similar flower shape and the inherent synergy of blue and yellow.

Platycodon grandiflorus,
Achillea spp.,
balloon flower, yarrow
Perennial blue balloon flower and golden yarrow combine with orange lilies in a summer meadow that sizzles with color.

Cistus × *purpureus*, *Ceanothus* spp.
rock rose, California lilac
The satiny pink flowers of rock rose and the soft gray-blue of ceanothus announce spring in West Coast gardens. Both shrubs rarely survive below-freezing temperatures.

purple

Majestic purple reigns as the garden peacemaker, marrying colors that often refuse to get along. The purple that streaks twilight's curtains evokes a melancholy stillness. More than any other color, purple gives the impression of texture. Purple is associated with a velvety feel, like the sueded petals of a pansy. Some people think purple too melodramatic and avoid it; others overindulge. But purple has a place in any garden.

playing with purple

- Purple foliage adds a compelling dimension to the garden. Consider purple varieties of ajuga, bergenia, smokebush, barberry, coral bells, snakeroot, geranium, and New Zealand flax.

- Because purple tends to get lost in the shade, pair it with a light-color companion, such as one with chartreuse or golden foliage.

- Smoky purples look their most regal in the fall, especially underplanting Japanese maples and other trees with brilliant red or gold leaves.

- Seek higher-power purples in vines: wisteria, clematis, sweet potato vine, and the dark-leaf grape (*Vitis vinifera* 'Purpurea').

Clockwise, from opposite top:

Viola × wittrockiana
pansy
This beloved annual perks up spring and fall gardens with its friendly faces. Pansies and other violas are naturally blue, purple, and lavender. Breeders raided the crayon box to give us pansies of every color.

Heliotropium arborescens
common heliotrope
Prized for its sweet vanilla-tinged fragrance, heliotrope develops dense flower heads of purple or white in summer. Bring it indoors for the winter.

Veronica hybrid
'Sunny Border Blue'
speedwell
Spikes of deep violet-blue stud this glossy-leaf perennial through the summer and into fall.

Scaevola aemula
fan flower
With pot-bursting vigor, this Australian native develops cascades of lavender-blue flowers.

Geranium hybrid
'Johnson's Blue'
cranesbill
A vital source of early-season blue-violet, this 18-inch-tall perennial blooms through the fall.

purple

Purple spans a wide range, from deep, velvety hues that appear almost black to pale periwinkle. Red-dominated hues of purple add suspense and drama to plantings. They also mediate, bridging the gap between related colors that form dissonant matches on their own, such as red and orange. Blue-violets anchor and visually blend brighter colors.

Purple's ideal partner, yellow, invariably lightens and brightens a scene. Purple and yellow announce spring's arrival in the blooms of bulbs and pansies. Yellow helps to solidify purple, whereas purple subdues yellow. This relationship of contrasts becomes more important in shade-dappled gardens, where purple would easily melt into the shadows without yellow to clarify it. White also stabilizes purple in shade gardens.

Other colors with yellow-dominant tints also flatter and define purple. Similarly, chartreuse plants make good partners. Purple and orange placed together send the color sparks flying in a match that's sultry and sophisticated.

Purple rounds out many effective trios. Plant it with chartreuse and pink for a sense of depth. When blended with blues and greens, it adds substance. Purple anchors combinations of red and gold, making them appear subtle and mysterious. Purple adds weight and value in a flower border. Use it as a shading tool to separate and define other colors.

Purple-leaf plants have become a huge trend in garden design. They offer a varied and versatile palette of trees, shrubs, and ornamental grasses, as well as perennials, annuals, and groundcovers. Incorporate purple-foliage plants into borders and backgrounds just as you would purple flowers to create a powerful sense of drama.

Clockwise, from opposite top:
Monarda didyma
bee balm
Reddish-purple bee balm, backed by a burgundy-leaf ornamental plum tree and edged with ornamental oregano, forms a dramatic summer scene.

Clematis × jackmanii
clematis
Vining clematis includes an array of species and hybrids—many with purple flowers. This large-flowering hybrid is one of the hardiest.

Thymus spp., *Alchemilla mollis*
thyme, lady's mantle
These hardy, sun-loving perennials meld in waves of purple, yellow, and green.

Campanula spp., *Achillea* spp.,
peach-leaf and clustered bellflowers, yarrow
Trim perennial bellflowers after their first bloom. You may see second flowerings that keep pace with yarrow's golden blooms.

Muscari spp., *Caltha palustris*
grape hyacinth, marsh marigold
Among spring's first flowering bulbs, this bold duo makes a splendid show.

lavender

Serene lavender brings a luster to the garden. It
holds just enough white to capture and reflect
light in a magical way. Beware of lavender's split
personality: In the warm light of sunrise or sunset,
it seems pink; in the cool light after sunset or in
shade, it appears blue. Like the herb that bears its
name, lavender stimulates the senses while it calms
the mind. It does the work of a garden mediator,
making peace among brasher colors. Give lavender
a chance to make an impression by combining it
with its relatives: violet, lilac, mauve, and purple.

Clockwise, from opposite top:

Clematis spp.
'Ramona' clematis
Plant this vining perennial near a tree or shrub and it will entwine itself through the branches. Protect the sensitive clematis crown from diseases and damage by planting it just above the soil line.

Lavandula angustifolia
English lavender
This fragrant herb requires a well-drained soil in a full-sun location. Cut back plants in spring to spur growth.

Allium senescens
flowering onion
The allium grows from a bulb and reaches heights of 3 to 24 inches. Lily stalks make strong living supports for the taller, top-heavy allium stems.

Dianthus spp., Nepeta × faassenii
'Bath's Pink' dianthus, catmint
This perennial duet blooms in early summer. Both plants have ground-hugging habits and do well in dry soils.

Petunia multiflora
petunia
Fertilize this showy annual often, and cut back leggy plants in midsummer to promote continuous cascades of fragrant flowers.

brush on the lavender

- Plant breeders haven't yet achieved a true blue rose, but lavender varieties come close. Consider pale 'Sterling Silver', 'Angel Face', and 'Lagerfeld'.
- The globe-shape flowers of onion family members, alliums and chives, span the lavender color spectrum. Try as many as you like.
- Lavender, in both name and hue, combines with silver- and gold-foliage plants to form borders that shimmer in the light.
- On the pinkish side of lavender, mauve's tonal ambiguities pose color-blending opportunities in the garden. Designers recommend using splashes of mauve flowers as dividers between deeper colors in a border.

ultimate yard & garden | **169**

lavender

As the most common flower color, lavender has many faces. It cools to a periwinkle blue in the flowers of *Vinca minor* and warms to a reddish mauve in clematis or pansy blossoms. Lavender abounds among the blossoms of herbs, from chives and hyssop to thyme, catmint, and sage.

Lavender forms harmonies with its cousins in the color spectrum: deep violet and magenta. Pale lavender creates soothing pastel scenarios when paired with white, pink, or pale yellow. Bluer shades of lavender shine when warmed by the company of complementary yellow-orange or peach. Planted near silver foliage, lavender looks luminous.

One weakness of lavender: It tends to fade into a dull haze en masse. Prevent this occurrence by interplanting it with bolder colors such as crimson or gold. Yellow makes a perfect partner. (Picture lavender and pale yellow violas that sport both colors in their spring blooms.) Chocolate brown foliage mixed with lavender flowers results in a spectacular marriage. At first blush, pink and lavender might seem too rosy a garden color scheme, but it's a combination that works. Lavender larkspur glows next to pink coneflower. Add white or sky blue to balance the pink tones. Mauve also goes well with cream, buff, gray, and pink.

Lavender enhances the fall garden's earth tones of bronze, orange, and gold with a touch of the ethereal, represented by perennial asters, fall crocuses, and aconites.

Clockwise, from opposite top:
Aster × frikartii
aster
Asters provide late-season shades of lavender in the garden. This compact variety doesn't need staking.

Rosa spp., Digitalis spp.
rose, foxglove
Biennial foxglove grows one year and blooms the next.

Iris × germanica
bearded iris (antique variety)
The iris lasts for decades in the garden. Dividing the rhizomes every few years keeps plants vigorous.

Lavandula spp., Artemisia spp., Cynara cardunculus
lavender, artemisia, cardoon
Mediterranean natives such as these perennials fare best in rocky soil and a sunny location.

Echinacea spp., Consolida ambigua
purple coneflower, larkspur
Sow annual larkspur seeds once; the plants will self-sow and return on their own in subsequent years.

ultimate yard & garden | **171**

white

White blends the intensity of all colors into light itself. Although white is not a color per se, it embodies simplicity and symbolizes purity. Crisp and refreshing on a summer afternoon, white also has a mysterious side that comes out to play by the light of the moon. As the evening deepens, white lights up. Many white-flowering plants have a fragrant bonus: Their intoxicating perfumes lure people as well as flying pollinators into the night garden.

Clockwise, from
opposite top:
Datura meteloides,
Nicotiana sylvestris
**datura, flowering
tobacco**
These tender plants
exude exotic perfumes.
But beware of datura
leaves and sap—
they're poisonous.

Anemone japonica
Japanese anemone
A tall white highlight in
fall gardens, this perennial
also flowers in pink and
mauve. It spreads quickly
in moist, enriched soils
and does especially well
in semishaded areas.

Ammi majus
Queen Anne's lace
This annual fills meadow
gardens with swaying
stalks of lace in mid- to
late summer. A relative
of the carrot, it has a
taproot and doesn't
transplant well, but it
reseeds gregariously.

Rosa hybrid
'Iceberg' rose
Dependable for landscape
uses such as hedging, this
Floribunda rose produces
multiflower branches of
delicate white all summer.

Nicotiana alata
jasmine tobacco
The frilled flower tubes
on this tall, hardy tobacco
fill the evening air with a
sweet, tropical perfume.
It thrives in partial shade.

ways to use white

- Highlight a focal point at the end of a path with white flowers or a white container.
- Among the most spectacular white-flower trees for landscapes: davidia, snowbell, magnolia, and dogwood. Some birches feature white trunks.
- Against the backdrop of a white fence, paint with the boldest plant colors possible, such as orange and scarlet.
- Light up your garden with white versions of these common plants: ageratum, cosmos, heliotrope, rhododendron, clematis, bee balm, and bleeding heart.
- Embroider white lace into your borders with these airy white flowers: rockcress, baby's breath, 'The Pearl' yarrow, and gooseneck loosestrife.

white
white

White brings out the true hues of any color with which it's paired. On the other hand, place a white flower next to green and it takes on a greenish tinge. The same phenomenon happens with yellow, pink, or blue. White has many personalities; it takes colorful companions to bring out white's myriad possibilities. Yellow-tinted white, or cream, harmonizes with almost every other flower color, as does variegated cream-and-green foliage.

An all-white garden cools and calms. Some gardeners design elegant white-flower refuges. A simple white palette paints borders with endless intrigue when white flowers mingle with a variety of leaf textures and colors: the bold with the fine (white coneflowers with lacy white yarrow), the

diminutive with the smooth (candytuft with hostas). Large white flowers, such as lilies or matilija poppy, lift the garden's horizon with simple, bold focal points. The delicate finery of baby's breath, Queen Anne's lace, or snow-in-summer breaks up reflected light for an effect of glimmering romance.

A popular choice for garden furniture and structures, clean, bright white says: "Welcome. Sit here. Walk this way."

Silver and silvery blue set off white, illuminating it. Although white provides a luminous divider for other colors, it can appear dimmed in gray climates. Avoid an overabundance of white in desert climates by subduing its harsh glare with equal amounts of silver and green.

Clockwise, from opposite top:
Convallaria majalis
lily-of-the-valley
A perennial groundcover bearing stalks of fragrant white bells. Dividing the plants every few years keeps them vigorous and productive. It thrives in shade.

Lavatera trimestris, Chrysanthemum parthenium
'Mont Blanc' mallow, matricaria
Annual mallow, a relative of the hollyhock, grows to 20 inches tall and produces abundant flowers, good for cutting. Matricaria prefers some shade and regular watering.

Rosa moschata, Allium multibulbosum
'Penelope' Musk rose, flowering onion
June brings the first blooms of this fragrant rose, timed with flower spheres of the tall allium. Hardy to Zone 5, 'Penelope' continues to bloom through the fall.

Leucanthemum × superbum, Lysimachia punctata
Shasta daisy, yellow loosestrife
Shasta daisies lighten up borders. The perennial loosestrife becomes a nuisance in damp soil.

silver

Silver adds a sprinkle of stardust to the most earthbound garden scenes. Spun from gray's whiter, less somber side, silver lightens and unifies. It binds plantings together in a dynamic play of light. Drifts of silver also act like storm clouds in the border, casting mysterious and ambiguous reflections, especially as the daylight dims. Silver-leaf plants, native to hot and sunny climes, look leaden in rainy areas; placed in a sunny spot, however, silver weaves endless enchantments.

strike a soft note with silver

- Grow these silver-leaf plants for their form: cardoon, clary sage, and globe thistle.
- Many silver-leaf plants, especially those with aromatic foliage, don't attract hungry deer. The deer-repelling list includes salvia, lavender, rosemary, and yarrow.
- Include plenty of silver spillers and cascading edgers, such as 'Silver Brocade' artemisia, snow-in-summer, silver thyme, lamb's-ears, germander, and lamium, in your borders and containers.
- Gray or silver embellishments, such as concrete statuary, mirrorlike water, or galvanized metal, act as ideal foils for plants.

Clockwise, from opposite top:
Artemisia hybrid
'Powis Castle' artemisia
Forming low mounds of ethereal silver lace, this perennial edges beds while highlighting and contrasting with masses of bright colors.

Senecio cineraria
dusty miller
The silver-sueded leaves of this annual weave texture into beds and containers. Remove flower stalks from this mounding plant to keep foliage vigorous.

Helichrysum petiolare
licorice plant
Winter hardy only in the warmest climates of Southern California and Florida, this fuzzy-leaf vining annual works well in potted schemes. Try chartreuse 'Limelight' or gold-and-green variegated forms.

Artemisia ludoviciana albula
'Silver King' artemisia
This tall, shrubby plant produces branches of aromatic foliage and enhances perennial borders with silvery, light-catching effects. Use it in dried arrangements and for wreath bases.

silver

Silver enchants green-dominated landscapes, visually underlining variations in greens that would otherwise go unnoticed. In hot, arid regions, silver stands in for green as the staple foliage color. Fuzzy silver-leaf plants have hairs that insulate against summer's heat and drought. This hairy coating gives silver its special reflective qualities.

Silver plants, whether the jagged leaves of an artichoke and its relatives, thistle and cardoon, or the wispy lace of 'Powis Castle' artemisia, weave fascinating textures into the border. Who can resist touching the plush leaves of lamb's-ears, a favorite silver edger?

Almost any color scheme has space for silver, but it blends especially well with pastels: pale pinks, blues, yellows, lavender, and white. Silver's ethereal appearance makes pastels stand out like lighted candles.

As a foil to brilliant-color flowers, silver cools and tames. It brings together hot hues that otherwise appear garish. Silver-splattered foliage plants, including pulmonaria and lamium, also put a shine in the border. They're even more valuable because of their tolerance for shade.

Clockwise, from opposite top:

Artemisia spp., *Echinacea purpurea*, *Eryngium* spp.
artemisia, 'White Swan' coneflower, sea holly
These hardy perennials thrive in the summer's worst heat. Harvest the artemisia foliage and sea holly flower heads for dried arrangements.

Geranium hybrid, *Pulmonaria saccharata*
'Johnson's Blue' cranesbill, 'Spilled Milk' lungwort
Both perennials form compact mounds, growing low to the ground. The lungwort flowers in early spring, but its foliage stays showy all summer.

Stachys byzantina
lamb's-ears
In a sunny location and adequately drained soil, it spreads vigorously. To keep the leaves large and showy, remove flower spikes when they form.

Artemisia spp., *Achillea* spp.
artemisia, yarrow
Both of these perennials have aromatic foliage and repel deer. They flourish in sunny, dry conditions. Remove faded flowers from yarrow to induce new blooms.

Pelargonium hybrid, *Helichrysum petiolare*
common geranium, 'White Licorice' helichrysum
Curl-leaf helichrysum grows assertively and dominates a container planting. Enjoy these annuals as long as they last.

rainbow

Vibrant, joyous colors flow throughout the garden and the seasons. The brilliant display starts with a burst of multicolor flowering bulbs in spring. By midsummer, it reaches a glorious crescendo. Bold and brilliant clusters of yellow, blue, red, purple, magenta, and more make harmonies and contrasts. Dense layers of color result in a horticultural masterpiece. Despite surprise combinations, there is a sense of balance in the patchwork garden. The overall effect is persistently cheerful.

colorful crowd

opposite: Almost every color earns the spotlight in this Canadian garden anchored by hardy roses, 'Morden Centennial' and 'Winnipeg Parks'. Drifts of allium, lemony 'Connecticut King' and pink 'Malta' Asiatic lilies fill in bare spots with midsummer color.

all-season rainbows

left: A skillful mix of perennials and annuals in layers achieves full and colorful effects. Perennials, such as the delphiniums and lilies, build the garden's form and architecture, whereas the annuals (dianthus, pansy, and geranium) expand it outward with bold splashes of summer color. The purple-flower edging of campanula and lobelia ties all the hues together.

growing rainbows

- Grow spectacular rainbow gardens by starting with garden gold: fertile soil, well amended with compost, rotted manure, and chopped leaves. Build raised beds with quality topsoil where the native soil is extremely poor (sandy, clayey, or otherwise poorly draining).

- Manage your horticultural masterpiece by planting dense layers of color. Group long-blooming plants according to their heights, as in a class photo: short in front, tall in back, others in between.

- Liberal plantings of green and white, working as neutral backgrounds or blenders, help make a multicolor scheme successful.

- Allow a couple of colors, such as blue and purple or pink, to dominate. Repeat plants and combinations in a border garden, to achieve dense splashes of color in patterns.

rainbow

Although they look casually composed, rainbow-color gardens disguise some careful sleight of hand. There's a knack to stringing colors, heights, and textures together into a unified design. Start with solid anchors in the form of roses and other shrubs that bring constant color into the border either via flowers or foliage or both. Then introduce perennials for form and color compatibility with the shrubs. Complete the garden's design with colorful outbursts of annuals.

Think of your color scheme as a patchwork quilt that comes together block by block. Design each block with annuals that echo or contrast with perennial flowers and foliage colors. Stitch each block to the next with threads of pink, white, silver, lavender, or green, those valuable linking colors.

Many garden designers use the technique of drift planting. This strategy takes triangular groupings of three, five, or seven plants of a single type, and preferably one color, and interweaves them with other triangles. For a more natural look,

plant list

1 foxglove, page 113

2 rose champion, page 118

3 red hot poker, page 117

4 petunia

5 cranesbill, page 114

6 ox-eye daisy, page 117

7 false sunflower, page 115

8 iris, pages 130–131

stretch out the far corner of the triangle so that the last plant grows into the adjacent grouping. Drifts fit best in large, open beds rather than narrow borders.

Finish the border's edges with unifying colors from flowers and from foliage plants. Foliage also comes in handy for filling bare spots next to roses or between young perennial plants.

If you need help planning your next garden, you can find the perfect combination of colors and plants in garden plans at **www.bhg.com/ bkgardenplans**

painting with plants
left and *opposite:* This garden illustrates a painterly technique: Blocks of color fit into an overall plan by harmonizing or contrasting with adjacent plants. Irises, red hot pokers, and red geraniums pour on the hot color, contrasting with cool-blossom petunias, foxgloves, daisies, and irises.

schemes
& themes

bold 186
pastel 192
foliage 196
tropical 204
color in the shade 210
monochromatic 214
two-color 222
trios 230
portable color 240

bold

unrestrained passion

Bold plant couples engage in the horticultural equivalent of passionate love affairs. Shocking! The usual rules fly out the window. Introduce one intense color to another and you have instant fireworks in the garden. The bold garden creates a sense of ongoing drama. It's a place where the most unexpected matches merge in sizzling synchronicity. Restrained gardeners who prefer neat-edge borders and pale palettes may accuse bold gardens of excess, but they earn a "Wow!" from others.

great combinations: magnificent magenta

Daring gardeners savor magenta's good vibrations and discover endless ways to contrast one of the boldest of the bold colors for stunning combinations, such as:

- magenta coneflower with silver artemisia
- hot pink English primrose with chocolate-leaf bergenia
- magenta cosmos with purplish bronze fennel
- lime green euphorbia with magenta-flower zinnia
- a deep pink rose with cinnamon-hue plume poppy
- magenta sweet William with burgundy astilbe
- magenta 'Ann Folkard' geranium with golden orange daylily

no-brakes borders

above: **A perennial border of bright delphinium, verbascum, *Anchusa azurea* 'Loddon Royalist', foxglove, and Maltese cross (*Lychnis chalcedonica*) appears beautifully balanced because all the flower colors register equal intensity.**

impromptu palette

right: **A mix of annual meadow flowers, including hot pink cosmos, striped mallow, blue bachelor's button, red flax, and yellow-and-burgundy coreopsis, displays a rich contrast of primary colors.**

bold

go for the bold

Bold garden designs take a fresh look at color and its capabilities. They dare to stretch color to extremes. The hottest pink juxtaposes with golden orange. Deep velvety purple pairs with vibrant yellow. Scarlet ignites when standing next to orange or magenta. A palette of rich, saturated hues dazzles the viewer from dawn to dusk.

The bold garden relies on color celebrities of equal intensity, used in dramatic vignettes. Give a brilliant pair the limelight by placing them front row center in the border, and then repeat the colors in the background, creating an echo of the original color match.

To discover a good match, get close and look at the whole blossom. No flower has an absolute single-color affiliation. Striping, patches, sheens, stamens, undertones, or throat all contribute to the flower's petal palette. One or more of these shades may harmonize with a likely partner. Also consider how the flower petals change color as they unfurl, then fade. Some roses may turn three or four different hues from bud to full bloom that could suggest color partners.

Plant shapes and bloom times also play a role in bold matches. A marriage of unusual forms creates major chemistry. For example, *Angelica archangelica* towers in a shade garden and frolicks spiritedly with the large, dark leaves and bright flowers of ligularia and gooseneck loosestrife.

partners that pop

right: **Blossoms of 'Purple Splendor' rhododendron and neon yellow perennial Iceland poppy would seem a jarring combination in an ordinary palette. But this bold design reaps the glowing payoffs of pairing yellow and purple—classically complementary. Both bloom in early spring.**

glowing pair

below: **The ember glow of 'Westerland' rose appears more luscious next to 'Wargrave Pink' geranium. A hardy Floribunda rose, 'Westerland' bears blooms that fade to peach, then to pink as they open, eventually almost matching the perennial geranium.**

Bold matches are limited only by the variety of flower colors available.

Success depends on timing. If you seek a color match and just can't find a flower partner that blooms at the same time, put foliage to work. The most breathtaking garden pairings often involve foliage understudies, not flower stars.

Plan your garden's bold color range for the intensity of light in its peak season. For instance, if plantings look their best in high summer, select the brightest colors possible so they won't fade in harsh sunlight. Tone down the color later by editing out plants or adding cooling white or silver plants as fillers among the brighter flowers.

bold

bold paint palette

Turn to perennials, shrubs, and bulbs to form your bold design's foundation. They'll give it stability with annual repeat performances.

Another bold approach involves a cast of thousands. Bright-flower summer annuals star in a mass planting that Victorian gardeners called bedding out; this bold scenario complements or contrasts colors. Or shades of the same color work in an analagous scheme. Mass plantings stop traffic with their sheer intensity of color. This type of bold garden requires lots of maintenance: fertilizing, watering, and removal of faded blooms keep the color showstopping.

Meadows result from nature's improvised mass plantings. Many a happy color accident happens when annual wildflowers mingle and turn up in unanticipated pairings. Predetermine the boldness of your meadow's color scheme by blending the seeds of your favorite hot hues. The meadow will perpetuate your brilliant scheme yearly by self-seeding.

Once you've got the knack of gardening boldly, surround yourself with color, overhead and all around. Think vertical and horizontal. Turn to trellises and arbors to raise the colors to new levels.

Gardens alone don't always instigate a bold design. Your color adventure may begin with a house color or an arbor painted in a favorite

south-of-the-border spice

above right: **The tropical leaves and volcanic blooms of cannas epitomize bold. Annual marigolds in a similar hot spectrum carry the brazen color scheme to the border's front. Choose cannas with striped foliage and neon-color flowers for maximum shock value.**

bold and beautiful

Use bold colors to enliven a scene, but remember to practice a modicum of restraint. Consider these outstanding color matches:

- Pair 'Royal Purple' smokebush with copper tulips or red Oriental poppies.
- Combine pink 'Silver Cup' lavatera with orange California poppies.
- Mingle red and gold daylilies, dahlias, and marigolds.
- Pair 'Goldsturm' *Rudbeckia* and *Aster × frikartii* 'Monch'. Include lamb's-ears as a calming device for the glowing duo.
- Mix summer bulbs: purple alliums and orange foxtail lilies.
- Contrast orange and yellow calendulas with flowering kale.

hue that calls for a coordinated garden. There again, foliage may provide all the highlights needed to support a bright house exterior or a hardscape accent. For example, a garden design featuring a complementary flower color mixed with white or silver will hold its own next to a periwinkle blue or lemon-yellow house.

When you go for a bold look, consider more than the plants. A warm-color fence, arbor, or chair, painted a rich hue of terra-cotta, apricot, yellow, or blue, brings out the brilliance of nearby, well-matched flower hues.

fiery pinnacles
left: **Massed plumes of gold, scarlet, and burgundy celosia, an annual bedding plant that thrives in summer heat, turn this border into red-hot real estate. Pink geraniums in the foreground take the tone down a notch.**

pastel

lighter shade of pale

For sheer delight, just add white. It gives pastel
hues their glow. Pale pinks, blues, lavenders, and
yellows light up shady places. Illuminated flowers
create islands of calm, soothing us with their
petal-soft lullabies. In gloomy climates, pastels
shine. Pastels offer visual refuge where the sun
beats down relentlessly. Fresh and quiet, pastel
gardens invite leisurely evening strolls
and restful interludes.

perennial oasis
*left: A free-flowing
perennial border
features an edge of
fragrant lavender and
phlox. Delphiniums
and annual pink
poppies also define
the color scheme.*

soft and scented
above: Catmint, campanula, verbena, and
lamb's-ears weave soft pastels into the
perfumed edge of a perennial bed.

whiter shades
opposite: Yarrow, catmint, lamb's-ears, and
'The Fairy' rose continue to glow as the sun
goes down. Snapdragon and larkspur enhance
the group.

pastel

painting with pastels

Pastels radiate most strongly in indirect light and on overcast days. Consider planting the subtle colors where the morning or evening light lingers. Swathes of pale-color flowers guide the way along a moonlit garden path. They brighten areas, such as a patio or deck, where you're likely to spend evening hours relaxing. Your palette can include more than flowers. The gleam of a pale tree trunk or silver leaves emanating light has just as much impact in a pastel garden's magic.

Against the backdrop of a brick wall or a dark, unpainted fence, pastel flowers gleam. They create a spotlight when planted around a focal point in the garden, such as statuary or a fountain, especially when viewed from a distance.

quiet corner

above right: **An understated blend of catmint, chamomile, salvia, and rose provides a relaxing spot to savor the aroma of herbs.**

spring scenario

right: **Spring and pastel color schemes seem to go together. The perennial groundcover *Phlox divaricata*, composes a pleasing complementary scheme with the flowering bulbs *Narcissus* 'Thalia' and a yellow jonquil.**

An entire contingent of peacemaking pastel colors tends to appear tepid when planted together. Add a little visual friction in the form of contrasting colors, along with framing greens and silvers, to separate the pastel shades.

Pastel flowers often offer alluring fragrance. Many flaunt sweet scents that announce the flowers' availability to insect and bat pollinators. Add pale-color roses, lilacs, magnolias, and honeysuckle to your garden schemes and enjoy their perfume as you stroll through the garden.

desert cool
left: **Three sturdy perennials for desert locales boast long-lasting color, including the 'Desert Sun' palo verde tree, *Agave americana*, and Mexican primrose (a groundcover).**

foliage

the essential leaf

Raindrop diamonds glimmer on a crinkled lady's mantle leaf. Silver foliage flutters along Russian olive branches. Emerging heather growth glows lime green.

Foliage has an essential and complex function in the plant world. It converts sunlight to life-sustaining sugars. In garden design, leaves assume equally important roles. They prolong a border's attractions through the season, giving it depth, flow, and personality. Whereas flash-in-the-pan flowers display vibrant colors timed to guide inbound pollinators, leaves put on a longer-running show.

Leaves build architecture. Used as hedging, groundcover, background, or striking specimen, foliage defines garden contours and skylines.

In fact, a planting limited to green palettes fascinates as much as a floor show of flamboyant blooms. Of all colors, green is viewed and perceived most easily. Using various shades of green only and interweaving delicate, airy foliage with coarser leaves creates an impressive tapestry that's easy on the eyes. In an all-green garden, a single plant with bold, dramatic foliage assumes the spotlight where flowers would usually stand. It has equal impact.

edible ornamentals
above: In the vegetable garden, contrasting green and burgundy leaf lettuces provide both spring highlights and harvests.

textured collage
right: Fine-texture sedum, thyme, and artemisia combine with juniper on a dry, sunny site.

foliar finery
opposite: A shady border gleams with skillfully composed silver fern, hosta, euphorbia, and columbine.

foliage

uncommon greenery

As if green's foliar offerings weren't riches enough, leaf hues span the entire spectrum. Foliage artists can dabble in shades from the smoky black of mondo grass (*Ophiopogon 'Nigrescens'*) and snake root (*Cimicifuga racemosa*) to the ghostly silver-white of *Artemisia lactiflora* and *Eryngium*. Purple, red, blue, silver, and golden foliage all supply pigments for composing vibrant garden masterpieces. Color-splattered leaves, such as those found in coleus and tovara, match almost any other leaf or flower color. Many plants also have contrasting leaf veins that coordinate with other foliage colors.

Every foliar hue has a special effect in the border. Green calms and soothes, which is why gardens designed mainly with greens offer welcome relief in urban settings and meditational refuges such as Japanese tea gardens. Blue and blue-green foliage, found in fescue and oat grass, create a cool

dappled drama

above right: In this green-and-cream scheme, dark, reddish, and rippled greens in the forms of geranium, *Euphorbia × martinii,* and hosta have even more impact next to variegated tovara.

no-bloom bouquet

right: Oxalis, or wood sorrel, oak fern, and *Heuchera* 'Palace Purple' with Hinoki false cypress in the upper right corner create a symphony of shapes.

and elegant link to other colors in a garden. Blue leaves mixed with purple-leaf plants and magenta flowers look spectacular.

Purple and burgundy foliage anchor garden borders, giving them solidity. The warm reds in coleus, maple trees, and ornamental grasses such as *Miscanthus* raise the pulse of foliar compositions with excitement and drama. Yellows have the same uplifting effect as sunshine in the border.

Gray and silvery gray foliage play magic leaf tricks. Although gray is a neutral mix of other colors, it reflects tints of complementary color partners. Next to red, it becomes slightly green. Paired with violet, it appears yellowed. Grays placed near orange have a blue tinge.

leaves afire
above: A tender annual, coleus inflames containers and beds with a color range from bronze and gold to purple and lime green. It grows indoors as a houseplant over the winter.

swirls and stars
left: Its swirling heads of chartreuse flower bracts make perennial *Euphorbia × martinii* a harmonious foliage partner for a bordeaux-color Japanese maple tree. These plants thrive in semishaded, moist soil.

ultimate yard & garden | **199**

foliage

preserve the pattern

Speckled, striped, or margined, multicolor leaf patterns serve up a little something different on the foliage color menu. Two-tone flowers are bicolored, whereas patterned leaves are variegated. The most common variegations express themselves in cream-, yellow-, or white-and-green foliage. Other, rarer, color patterns include the silver streaks in *Heuchera, Tiarella, Pulmonaria,* and *Lamium* leaves, as well as the rainbow splatters found in Japanese maple hybrids, leucothoe, and other plants.

Vegetable leaves also display wildly variegated colors. Be sure to include red-speckle leaf lettuces, the frosted blue-green and lavender found in ornamental kale and cabbage, plus 'Rainbow' chard in your foliar palette of special effects.

Overall, variegated plants lighten and refresh a border, especially when blending green and white or green and cream. Plants naturally develop multicolor leaf mutations; then plant breeders discover, preserve, and copy them. Due to the instability in a hybrid's genetic makeup, it takes extra effort to help these plants thrive in the garden and sustain their showy leaves. Adequate fertilizer and plenty of sunlight preserve the showy foliage. Cut off flower stalks of variegated plants, such as polka-dot plant (*Hypoestes*), coleus, lamb's-ears, ornamental cabbage, flowering kale, lettuce, and basil, to ensure leaf vigor and continuous color.

glowing foliage

right: A variegated euphorbia pairs with 'Royal Cloak' purple barberry and chartreuse-leaf *Geranium sinense* in a hardy planting that furnishes almost year-round color.

radiant tapestry

left: A planting of perennial variegated golden ribbon grass, purple-leaf coral bells, and bergenia radiates with purple and gold-tone harmonies. The design works well as a front-of-the-border display or by providing foliar footlights under trees.

taking a shine to shade

below left: Silver sets the tone for this low-growing mélange of gray-green perennials, including *Pulmonaria*, *Anthriscus sylvestris* 'Ravens Wing', and *Arabis caucasica*, or rockcress. White florets of the *Arabis* and *Anthriscus* pose dainty counterpoints to the foliage.

multipurpose herb

below: The aromatic leaves of 'Tricolor' sage have culinary uses, and the plant edges flower beds with ornamental highlights.

foliage

a garden gold rush

You might associate yellow flowers with the sunny peak of summer, but golden foliage imparts instant warmth to a landscape year-round. Especially valuable in regions dominated by cloudy skies and diffused light, gold-leaf plants supply the missing sunshine. Shady areas, a frequent challenge in mature landscapes, take on a glow with golden foliage. You have many options when it comes to painting the border gold. The gold-tone leaf has become a focus in recent breeding and gilds everything from groundcovers and vines to trees.

Most foliage shows a hint of gold when first emerging in spring. Most tree and shrub foliage turns to burnished gold, prompted by fall frosts. Conifers, including *Chamaecyparis*, wear winter cloaks of gold-tinged green.

Other gold nugget plants include the most popular ornamental grasses for shade, *Hakonechloa macra* 'Aureola' and sedges. Are you bold enough for bamboo? Consider the 'Golden Goddess' and yellow-groove bamboos.

Pale gold and green-and-gold variegated hostas, reportedly more tolerant of sun, include 'Frances Williams' and 'Gold Standard'. Gold-splashed varieties of ligularia, a large-leaf perennial, offer other options for shade. Among vines, 'Gold Net' variegated honeysuckle goes airborne with golden foliage. Low to the ground, golden creeping Jenny and *Veronica repens* fill in gaps with their sunshine.

rivers of gold

right: **In this colorful composition of 'Bowles Golden' tufted sedge, *Anthriscus* 'Ravens Wing', 'Aurea' barberry, variegated hosta, and 'Negrita' purple tulips, blooms provide contrast rather than focus. This perennial painting repeats itself each spring.**

golden spikes

above: Gold-digging plants, such as variegated moor grass *(Molinia caerulea 'Variegata'),* 'Norton's Gold' oregano, and 'Aurea' barberry, will glow in just about any type of soil. A full-sun exposure enhances their gold coloration.

spend gold wisely

All that glitters doesn't necessarily pan out in a garden's design. Here are some locations where gold plants will pay high dividends:

- As an underplanting around trees and shrubs in shady areas.
- Contrasting and highlighting purple-leaf perennials and shrubs.
- Mingling with silver-variegated plants such as lungwort. Gray leaves cast a violet glow over gold and soften its impact.
- Blending with yellow- and green-variegated leaves, gold foliage looks as pretty and prominent as soft-yellow flowers.

tropical

touch of the tropics

Anything is possible when horticultural tradewinds bring adventurous plants to your yard. Banana leaves rise on the prairie; plumeria thrives in Iowa. Tropicalissimo warms the blood and the border with plant fantasies come true.

Dramatic structure and colors tip a garden's design into the tropical zone. The tiger-stripe foliage of a canna, and the vibrant lime, pink, and purple of coleus leaves, put the fun back in gardening. Victorian-era gardens popularized summer beds where circus-color menageries of exotic plants romped. Tropical plants seem at home in any climate. When the sun heats up, their growth accelerates into junglelike luxuriance.

hot and cold

above right: Sedum 'Mohrchen', with its rosy brown flowers and chocolatey stems, colors a perennial vignette with purple fleabane (*Erigeron karvinskianus*) that's tropical in flavor but hardy in cold climates.

tropical punch

right: In mai tai colors, *Dahlia* 'Simplicity' and *Alstroemeria* 'Beatrix' warm the border with summer flowers. In cold climates, dig up their tubers after the first frost and store them indoors through the winter.

jungle flora

opposite: A flock of flamingo-like striped cannas brings this perennial border into bold focus. Tropical touches include cape fuchsia, nicotiana, and fiery-flower potentilla and crocosmia. Butterfly bush, meadow rue, purple sage, lysimachia, and lady's mantle blend cooling touches of lavender and chartreuse.

foliage fever

Savvy gardeners value many tropical natives for their flamboyant foliage. Coleus, an annual in most North American climates, offers hundreds of varieties in shades of kiwi green, magenta, gold, burgundy, and white. Sun-tolerant varieties with thicker leaves have recently debuted.

Cannas, grown from rhizomes, sport bold leaves often striped in gold and topped with bright red, orange, yellow, or pink flowers. Another tuberous plant, caladium, develops arrowhead-shape leaves in pink, red, and green. Angel-wing and Rex begonias also add speckled and striped foliage to the tropical palette. Elephant's ear (*Colocasia*) contributes massive, lofty leaves in deep purple, gold, or green.

The unusual blooms of flowering plants from the tropics of Africa and South America, when

captivating coleus
below: Like many tropicals, coleus responds well to an occasional deadheading. Pinch off their lavender flower spikes for a continuously showy crop of leaves.

planted in borders or containers, form delicate contrasts against flamboyant leaves. Abutilon's inverted bell flowers attract hummingbirds by the droves, as do the trumpet blooms of *Phygelius* (cape fuchsia). *Brugmansia*, or angel's trumpet, boasts dramatic flowers with a sweet fragrance. Overwinter these torrid-zone plants indoors.

Hot oranges, reds, and yellows for painting tropical palettes come from nasturtium and Mexican sunflower *(Tithonia)*. Annual and perennial salvias supply blues, reds, and purples. Summer bulbs that also fit the tropical motif include crocosmia, dahlia, and *Eucomis*, or pineapple lily.

tropical's subtle side
left: Melianthus major, or honey bush, poses with golden elephant's ear and 'Fascination' dahlia. It grows as an annual in cold climates.

tiger tale
left: Growing to an imposing 6 feet, 'Bengal Tiger' (also known as 'Praetoria') is one of the showiest cannas, with apricot-orange flowers appearing successively from midsummer to the first frost. Potting summer-flowering tubers and bulbs keeps them portable and easy to move indoors to overwinter.

tropical illusions

The best-kept secret about tropical gardens is that not all the players need hail from exotic locales. Think large and dramatic foliage plus bold color, and you'll end up with hundreds of plants that are growable in your garden all year despite long, cold winters. Glossy groundcovers with a lush habit include hardy arums and asarums. You can't beat *Acanthus, Gunnera,* or *Rheum* for leafy architecture, and all these perennials survive cold winters. The imposing leaves of catalpa and magnolia trees have a tropical feel, yet they're quite hardy. Dutchman's pipe, trumpet vine, and hardy passionflower display a junglelike vigor, and the vast bamboo and fern families number several cold-hardy species in their ranks.

Among succulents, sedum, sempervivum, yucca, and prickly pear cactus can weather cold winters. *Melianthus,* a fringed silvery shrub from mountainous Africa, ranks high on the list of tropical wannabes. It has an imposing structure and a crowd-pleasing color that makes it an outstanding companion plant. New Zealand flax (*Phormium*) has multicolor straplike leaves that make good focal points in tropical-theme borders. Some *Phormium* hybrids are hardy to Zone 7.

After the final frost in spring, plant showy annuals to fill gaps in a tropical-look garden. Use castor bean, plume poppy, and cleome for striking height or form. Annual vines grown from seed,

sassy dancers

right: Think of potted tropicals as living flower arrangements or the Carmen Mirandas of containers. Weekly feeding and removal of spent flowers help keep coleus, caladium, petunia, lantana, pentas, and canna looking lush all summer.

such as purple hyacinth bean, scarlet runner bean, or black-eyed Susan vine, rise up quickly and entwine structures in junglelike lushness.

Houseplants that have languished on the windowsill all winter can also be exported to add color to tropical borders. Hibiscus, palm, and others bring Hawaiian-shirt shades and shapes into temperate gardens. Make an easy fall transition to indoors by keeping a group of potted houseplants on the patio or deck, or gather them in a corner of the garden that offers late-day shade.

tropical leaf motif

left: A potted garden showcases assorted wavy foliage of elephant's ear and caladium punctuated by knobs of lavender allium and green amaranth spikes. All except the annual amaranth are bulbs to be saved for the next year's planting.

quick-and-easy tropical decor

- String up a hammock or sky chairs in place of traditional loungers. Choose rattan, wicker, or bamboo furniture.
- Use large-print floral fabrics in bright colors for a tablecloth, napkins, cushion covers, or a folding screen.
- Replace a standard patio umbrella with a *talapa* (a thatch reed umbrella designed to withstand harsh coastal conditions).
- Select bamboo as a building material for structures of all sorts, from plant supports and fencing to an arbor or a pergola.

color in the shade

shady propositions

The shade of established trees and tall buildings invites opportunities of shadowy splendor. Enjoy a colorful shade garden by choosing from a vast population of shade-loving perennials, annuals, and tropicals.

Container gardens make it easy to paint by number in the shade. Coleus, Persian shield (*Strobilanthes*), caladium, lisianthus, polka-dot plant, and ornamental sweet potato vine (*Ipomoea batatas*) take to the shady life with zeal, growing up and spilling over in no time. Mix them with the brilliant blooms of tuberous begonia, New Guinea impatiens, vinca, white or blue browallia, pentas, abutilon, and fuchsia to create memorable masterpieces that illuminate the shade.

Successful potted gardens often break the rules about who can live where. Sun lovers may thrive as temporary tenants in partial shade, especially if you meet their needs for heavy feeding and flower grooming. If plant colors start to flag, move the container to a sunnier spot.

One other rule made to be broken pertains to the pots themselves. In shade, colorful containers should stand out and be counted. Use roomy, bright-color vessels pierced with drainage holes to spotlight flashy, exotic plants.

made for shade
right: Tiered container plants stage a wall of blazing color on a shady deck. The gathering represents an annual who's-who of shady horticulture. Ornamental sweet potato vine, coleus, Persian shield, and New Guinea impatiens feature prominently with sun-loving zinnias and lantana.

color in the shade

shadow dancing

Shaded ground can glow with color from both flower and foliage gems. Start by layering shades of green, and place a variegated or yellow-leaf plant at the center of a grouping. Frame a green-and-white hosta, for example, with a background of silvery ferns. Take a tip from Asian gardens by incorporating one flowering plant, such as camellia or rhododendron, as a seasonal accent in a sea of tranquil green.

Just a few of the colorful and textural foliage options for shade include *Aquilegia, Dicentra,* or *Nandina* for delicacy; boxwood, euonymus, or daphne for highlights; *Acanthus,* hellebore, and gunnera for structure; and *Lamium, Pulmonaria,* and *Houttuynia* for contrast. Employ fine-texture ivies, *Schizanthus,* and climbing hydrangea to ascend the walls, adding extra dimensions of green, silver, and white. Climbing bleeding heart, *Dicentra scandens,* bears dainty yellow flowers in partial shade.

Ornamental grasses illuminate and soften semishady garden edges, spilling over walkways. Sedges, golden hakone grass, and feather reed grass all tolerate shady locales.

Hardscaping also helps illuminate shady areas. Walkways and stepping-stones in pale flagstone or concrete bring a gleam to shadowy paths. Water features, mirrors, and reflective gazing balls open up shaded areas, adding flashes of brilliance.

lighten up

right: Light-color flowers, foliage, and pavers make this dim enclosure appear warm and expansive. The fountain and pool reflect a bit of light too.

fantastic footlight

left: A gazing ball catches and throws back sunlight, magically opening a shady area in a double exposure. Salvia spikes form a flattering frame for the silver sphere.

texture trove

below left: A montage of shade-thriving perennials includes ground-carpeting *Pulmonaria*, *Pachysandra*, columbine, hosta, and silver fern.

1,000-watt color in the shade

- Supplement garden color with large pots of brilliant blooms (petunia, begonia) and foliage (caladium, coleus).
- Concentrate on warm and vivid contrasts in your shady color scheme, especially reds and burgundies with yellow and chartreuse.
- Furnish a shady corner with chairs, pots, or structures painted a glowing color.
- Include reflective features, such as light-tone concrete statuary, a fountain, or a small pool of water.
- Use ground lighting to set the place aglow after sunset. Dangle lanterns in trees.

monochromatic

one-on-one

Single-color gardens show as much boldness and flair as the most elaborately matched schemes. A one-color strategy frees you to master the brushstrokes of form and texture. It also allows enough elbow room to explore a single-color palette's potential in pale and deep shades.

Consider green, for example; it doesn't fatigue the eye. It offers an endlessly varying palette, from true green, gray-green, and blue-green to purple-green and yellow-green. Each has a different impact.

In small, all-green spaces, paint with plenty of blue-green plants. Blue-tint leaves have the same deepening effect as blue flowers. Blue hostas and Solomon's seal visually widen shady areas with their broad leaves. Rue, thalictrum, and *Rosa glauca* weave lacy texture into all-green gardens.

Color contrasts in a monochromatic garden rouse a simple palette and make it sing. Purple-green looks dramatic when rubbing elbows with yellow-green, for example. Blend pools of true green or silvery green in between.

green unlimited

right and *below:* This pond garden has a sweeping vista in a palette of greens. The statue, trellis, and rocks add contrasting textures.

plant list

1 boxwood

2 nandina

3 blue oat grass, page 129

4 japanese privet

5 siberian iris, pages 130–131

6 calla lily

7 rose

8 sea pink, page 107

monochromatic

illuminating white

Turn a garden into a classic, using a palette of white. Widely available in flowers, foliage, and garden decor, white projects a refreshing clarity. Paint with white to expand your garden's visual boundaries just as you would brush on white to enlarge interior rooms. Dull or shady areas, especially, benefit from white's sparkle.

Include any variation of white, from buff to silver, to give your white garden interest beyond the pale. Light pastel colors blend well too, so highlight white with pale peach, yellow, lavender, and pink. In an all-white garden, texture becomes all important in establishing individual plant identities. Combine thick, satiny petals with sheer

evening glow

above right: **Gleaming candlelight and glowing annual** *Zinnia angustifolia* **team up with ribbon grass and artemisia to illuminate a gravel path.**

summer whites

right: **An all-white arrangement of phlox, hydrangea, baby's breath, and 'Fair Bianca' rose, accented with silver lamb's-ears, reaches its flowering peak in midsummer but looks fresh and tranquil all season. The arbor adds architectural white.**

ones; set off large, showy blooms by framing them with feathery flowers or foliage.

All-white gardens shine as the sun goes down. Place a fragrant white border where it will captivate at twilight. Some white fragrant bloomers to place along paths and lean against arbors include peonies, nicotiana, moonflowers, phlox, and lilies. Include jasmine or stephanotis in warm climates.

Garden elements reflect the same glow as white plantings. Pale-color gravel, stepping-stones, arbors, and picket fences put a permanent luster on white gardens.

shade paint

left: **Like white paint indoors, white wood in a dark garden corner creates a sense of space. Crisp white clematis and variegated bishop's weed (*Aegopodium*) enhance the effect.**

monochromatic

heat waves

Florists and gardeners share this successful technique: An arrangement composed around a single color epitomizes elegance. Monochromatic plantings designed from the spectrum's warm side leave memorable impressions.

Textural interplay heightens the drama of a one-color garden. The bold trumpets of orange daylilies, for example, dance bloom to bloom with delicate plumes of pale peach astilbe and glowing wands of 'Lucifer' crocosmia. Strategic plant location also heightens the impact of monochromes. Place loose or open-branched plants toward the border front to allow a view through of more substantial flowers beyond. This down-in-front framing strategy helps create the same sense of suspense and depth as a bend in the path or a long view through an arbor.

Another design technique involves planting a bed of annuals in monochromatic bands. Beds of multicolor annuals can confuse rather than compel. If limited to a single color and specific varieties, however, the planting has stronger impact.

Light intensity also heightens monochrome drama. An all-yellow border dazzles under softly lit, overcast skies or when located in a shady nook. Orange or red schemes look stunning poised against a west-facing view, where the sinking sun backlights them with a fiery aura.

light a fire
right: **A rich-hue band of coleus spreads like fire across the border and reflects the daylilies' colors. The warm-color scheme enlivens the neutral-tone house.**

golden glow
left: A sunny border puts yellow's synergy to work by combining daylilies, heliopsis, and coreopsis. Yellow corydalis, trollius, and golden hosta offer options for a border in the shade.

peachy pizzazz
below: A molten flow of orange dahlias, nasturtium, rose, and salpiglossis, contrasted with chartreuse euphorbia and white feverfew, flatters the warm tones of the brick border edging.

monochromatic

purple majesty

Purple reigns supreme in the garden. The color of cabbages and kings plants peace between louder colors and deserves garden homage to its quiet tones. An all-purple or all-lavender garden would appear downright melancholy. But various purple hues, mingled with silver or gold foliage and amplified with red or orange counterpoints, would emanate luminous splendor.

Make a purple planting more dynamic by playing every note in the purple range: violet, mauve, periwinkle, deep reddish purple, and purplish black. Give lavender the role of blender, as in multicolor gardens.

Once you've established a purple foundation, add contrasts. Surround purple plants with lighter silver and brighter gold to keep them in focus. Golden cultivars of conifers, flowering shrubs, and

autumn mists

above right: **Asters, phlox, grasses, and woolly lamb's-ears seem to float above the ground, but the solid green of the bergenia leaves anchors the plantings.**

quiet scene

right: **The lavender of catmint and *Verbena bonariensis* below a red Japanese maple would look somber without the softening effect of lamb's-ears and golden hops. The lone pink poppy adds a lighthearted note.**

ornamental grasses stand out next to purple plants. Mingle purple smokebush and a purple-flowering *Buddleia* with a golden elderberry or 'Golden Sword' *Yucca flaccida*.

Silver companions shine in the presence of purple and bring out its mysterious side. Pair lamb's-ears with aster, artemisia with a lavender rose, and autumn crocus with silvery blue fescue to create ethereal vignettes.

Avoid monotony in purple schemes by weaving in one emphatic color. Use just a few plants that accent the flower centers of purple blooms or the veining of purple leaves. A shout of fiery red or flashes of brilliant orange cast purple in a flattering light. One hot pink spotlight in a contrasting shape also works as the exclamation point in an all-purple statement.

purple pleasers

- groundcovers: 'Burgundy Glow' *Ajuga*
- tropicals: 'Blackie' ornamental sweet potato vine, lantana, coleus, Persian shield
- perennials: 'Vera Jameson' sedum
- herbs: 'Purpureum' bronze fennel, 'Dark Opal' basil, 'Berggarten' sage, perilla
- vegetables: eggplant, 'Lollo Rosso' lettuce, 'Royal Burgundy' bush beans, 'Purple Passion' asparagus, 'Ruby Perfection' cabbage

fall sunset scheme
left: Ageratum 'Blue Horizon', cosmos, and aster show the luminiscent quality of lavender with colorful support from the grenadine-color chrysanthemum.

two-color

white weddings

Combined with any color, white has the impact of a mint sprig in lemonade: It adds an edge of refreshing crispness. White's chameleon-like nature also makes it the color companion valued most in the garden. Next to warm yellows and reds, white softens. With cool blue and purple, it appears frosty and defined. Free from color, white assumes whatever tint stands next to it.

Drifts of white in a red-hot border lower the temperature. A red and white scheme strikes a balance between excitement and relaxation. For a fresh-faced look, pair yellow or orange flowers with white blooms that have warm-color centers.

Planted next to recessive blue flowers or foliage, white shines like a lightbulb in bloom, yet the overall effect is quiet and harmonious. Whites drawn from either variegated foliage or flowers become highlights when interspersed among green, particularly in a shady setting. Combined with pink, lavender, or silver, white appears enchanting. White roses peeking out among lavender phlox, or lavender clematis draped on a white arbor, look stunning at twilight.

shades of nightfall

right: Oakleaf hydrangea, snapdragon, and sweet alyssum star in this circular garden, but nuances of lavender scabiosa, campanula, delphinium, and salvia soften the potential glare of the mostly-white scene.

blue and white classic

opposite: White flowers would ordinarily fade into a white house, but the peegee hydrangea outshines a blue spruce standard, a dwarf Alberta spruce, blue salvia, and variegated plectranthus.

two-color

midas touches

When yellow joins other flower colors, the scene invariably lightens and brightens. Yellow boosts the border with the visual equivalent of laughter. It shimmers in shady places.

Purple tones, from purplish green to lavender, respond warmly to a yellow partner. Bright spring yellows frequently pair up with purple and blue blooms. But what about a late-spring follow-up act of yellow peonies (*Paeonia lutea*) with purple-leaf rhododendrons; lavender irises and gold *Veronica repens*; or 'Baggesen's Gold' honeysuckle and hardy ginger (*Roscoea purpurea*)?

Use yellow shrubs as ornamental highlights in flower borders. They'll add spark to mellow monochromes of purple or pink. Many gardeners greet the spring with bright yellow forsythia, but other shrubs spread wonderful buttery color in plantings. For shade, *Kerria japonica* bears single or double popcorn flowers of pure gold against vivid green stems. *Kirengeshoma*, a large perennial, and *Rhododendron luteum* twinkle with pale yellow flowers, while mahonia glistens with sprays of bright yellow. In sunny gardens, witch hazel and broom (*Cytisus*) flower in early spring. Golden-leaf varieties of weigela, elderberry, caryopteris, and barberry enhance borders with their glow.

Yellow and white form a winning combination that glows dramatically when reflected in water.

border light

right: Yellow daylilies and coreopsis add sparkle to a palette of purples, including smokebush, coneflower, petunia, and phlox. The scheme would appear muddy without yellow's light and cheerful touch.

A midsummer border could pair fragrant yellow-throated *Lilium regale* and 'Stella de Oro' daylily, or white astilbe and a gold-variegated ornamental grass. By adding 'Goldfinch' goldenrod or 'Garden Sun' helenium and white mums, the gold and white show lasts through the fall.

Many daisylike yellow flowers provide late-summer color. Sustain the sunshine of coreopsis, helenium, and black-eyed Susan by snipping off faded flowers after their first bloom. A second flowering soon follows.

faces in the clouds
below: **A mass of purples and yellows visually softens the bronze sundial. Two-tone pansies emanate personality, as lavender and lady's mantle form clouds of summer color.**

two-color

red-hot matches

Reds highlight otherwise subdued colors so they'll be noticed. Warm colors intensify when stationed next to red. Cool classics, such as green and white, suddenly look fresh and sparkling when a dash of red is applied among them.

Green, especially, gains vibrancy in the company of its complement: red. The green-and-red leaves of caladium or *Euphorbia × martinii* look spectacular combined with deep red flowers, including tuberous begonia, fuchsia, and *Lobelia cardinalis*. Unusual green flowers, such as hellebore or bells of Ireland, go well with reddish-foliage plants. Rich reds, found in roses and peonies, create beautiful relationships with the chartreuse leaves and flowers of lady's mantle or cushion spurge. Any green or chartreuse shrub glows in the company of a red Japanese maple.

Red and yellow make a happy blend of two warm temperaments. Such strong colors should register equal intensity to combine successfully, golden yellow with bright red, for example. When yellow flowers sport contrasting red centers or markings, such as daylilies, tulips, *Coreopsis tinctoria*, gaillardia, and helenium, the bond grows even stronger.

Red adds a pulse to all-white plantings. White and red roses provide a classic look among dark green foliage. A ribbon of white mums winding around a fall-reddened tree or shrub looks exquisite. Likewise, Japanese blood grass mixing with 'Snowbank' boltonia or white asters create a stellar combination.

formal with a flair

right: **Bands of red impatiens and gladiolas, plus other red accents, enliven a formal scheme.**

dynamic duets

- deep blue with peach: delphinium and pale peach Oriental poppy
- silver-blue and ruby red: blue spruce entwined with 'Niobe' clematis
- burgundy flowers and silver foliage: dahlias planted around cardoon
- red and gold: *Astrantia* paired with sedge
- deep purple and pale yellow: purple coleus with trailing light-yellow lantana
- orange with buff: 'Paprika' yarrow and *Stipa tenuissima* (an ornamental grass)

spicy hot
below: A timber-edge bed warms to a spring bulb-and-annual medley of yellow and red ranunculus, Temari verbena, calendula, geranium, stock, Dutch iris, and white creeping zinnia.

two-color

two-part harmonies

Side by side on the color wheel, reds and oranges
also bond in the border. To ensure compatibility,
select reds that run to warm crimson rather than
cool burgundy. Red flax or poppies mingled with
orange butterfly weed creates jewel-like effects in
a meadow garden setting. A mix of red and peach
dahlias sizzles in a hot-weather color scheme,
especially if the 'Bishop of Llandaff' dahlia, with its
chocolate-color foliage, fills the red role. 'Lady in
Red' annual salvia, paired with nasturtiums and
'Peaches 'n' Cream' verbena, strikes equally warm
notes up front in the border or arranged in a pot.

Pink and white plantings also radiate warmth,
but with pastel overtones. Both colors get along
with any other. Paired with each other, however,
the combo is as delicious as strawberries and
cream. Soft, satiny pink 'Bonica' roses spilling
over a white picket fence couldn't ask for any
better company than pink-and-white alstroemeria,
magenta penstemon, and the starry white
counterpoint of *Leucanthemum paludosum*.

For a slightly warmer look, introduce yellow
to your favorite deep pink flowers. Gold foliage
provides the least intrusive way to play up the
color chemistry. Use *Helichrysum* 'Limelight' to set
off magenta petunias, for instance. Rosy phlox
and pink coneflowers create striking pairs with
golden-flower perennials.

rosy rabbit refuge

right: Purples and pinks hit it off in a border
filled with geranium, lobelia, sweet alyssum,
barberry, daisy, and 'The Fairy' rose. Golden
arborvitae focal points, along with the bold
foliage of strawberry, sedum, and others, keep
the rosy scene from appearing too precious.

sizzling slope

below: **Cascades of annual nasturtiums and million bells, plus impatiens, dahlias, and *Cuphea*, warm the brick walls of a terraced garden with hot points of color. The barberry below and pale climbing rose above contribute structure. Green pots and foliage provide continuity among the spice-color flowers.**

Closely related on the color wheel, pink and purple make a successful team in the garden. Annual *Salvia viridis* furnishes both colors on spiky stalks. Purple larkspur pairs beautifully with pink poppies, and lisianthus goes with pink 'Garden Bride' baby's breath. Violet clematis and pink roses paint a rich, two-tone portrait. Purple basil makes a stunning foliage filler in a bed of pink blooms. An early-spring scene features pink creeping phlox and purplish-blue forget-me-not. Pink autumn crocus and purple-bronze *Ajuga* combine for fall.

Make purple pop by adding an orange partner, such as tall zinnias accompanying 'Purple Rain' salvia, or match blooms of lavender bellflower with coral 'Elfin Pink' penstemon.

trios

three's company

The whole is greater than the sum of its parts. This adage proves true in the garden where pairs of companionable plants are common. But whereas two are good, three can be better.

When a three-part color harmony relies solely on flowers, its timing must be in sync. Group three plants that should bloom about the same time in the season to make an effective trio. A late-spring design could include Oriental poppy, iris, and delphinium. Plan late-blooming replacements and extend the trio into midsummer. Let blue larkspur take over for the iris and add annual poppies to fill in after the Oriental poppy foliage fades.

What's the easiest way to start thinking in threes? Take a favorite flowering shrub, such as a rose or a long-blooming perennial, then showcase it with two foliage partners. Select foliage for its shape but also for factors such as fall color and tones that pick up color in the flowers' petals, stamens, or markings. Many flowers have golden stamens, so gold foliage often makes a good partner for them.

thinking in threes

- Plant in threes. Practicing this old garden adage results in a fully mature-looking spread of one plant variety when adding new plantings.
- Decorate in threes. Choose one main color and add two accent colors to create a color scheme that plays on harmonies or contrasts.
- Accessorize in threes. Arrange colorful pots or other decorative elements in groups of three or five for the best results.

flower power

above: Subtle color paints this grouping of a 'New Dawn' rose, *Geranium pratense*, and *Euphorbia* 'Mrs. Robb's'. The geranium flowers early to midsummer; the rose blooms all summer. A favorite Climber, the rose grows up to 10 feet high and is hardy to Zone 5.

petal collage

right: Two perennials and 'Graham Thomas', a Shrub rose, combine in a trio of silky-petal pastels. The lavender *Campanula persicifolia*, or peach-leaf bellflower, flourishes in a sunny spot. Cut back the stems after the first bloom to encourage new shoots. Pink 'Proteus' clematis features double flowers and tolerates cold winters to Zone 4.

trios

triple treats

Triple the potential fragrance of roses by partnering them with small- and medium-height herbs. Versatile herbs possess aromatic appeal and they repel pests and soilborne diseases. Herbs also function as border edgers, perennial partners, and background choruses. Many of them have culinary uses too.

Sprays of bright-blue borage flowers and their prickly silver-green leaves add a glow to blooming companions. Borage makes a winning partner with peach and yellow roses. It grows easily and rapidly from seed.

Place a fine-texture haze of color behind brilliant flowers with angelica, bronze fennel, tarragon, or a taller artemisia, such as 'Silver King'. Add chartreuse highlights, especially among red or orange flowers, with dill or an arbor of golden hops. Artemisia, lavender, rosemary, and clary sage shine silver spotlights on white and pink or white and lavender combos.

For edging color and texture, rely on parsley, chives, sage (especially the purple and tricolor varieties), and globe basil. Creeping varieties of thyme and mint pave edges and walkways with shades of gold, purple, and green.

pink portrait

right: 'Earth Song', a Grandiflora rose, rises with fragrant dianthus and thyme at its feet. Foliage on the early-summer-blooming perennials stays attractive all summer. The rose bears double blooms and grows to 5 feet.

terrific trio

left: Bee balm, lavender, and yarrow sustain a colorful summer border of perennial herbs. They also boast fragrance and a history as herbal remedies. The plants dry well for wreath making and other decorative uses.

easy threesie

below: Spanish lavender, purple sage, and 'Doone Valley' thyme form a striking and aromatic group in hot sun and dry soil. *Lavandula stoechas* flowers in early summer, with hardiness to Zone 7.

ultimate yard *&* garden |

trios

spring combos

Spring wears a mostly subdued color wardrobe, except for the bright yellow exultations of daffodils and forsythia. The season is typically depicted in soft pink, lavender, and blue. These three pastel colors work well together and separately when mixed with yellow-green, silver, and the white of blossoming fruit trees. In spring, flowering bulbs appear first, often wearing complementary shades of purple or lavender and yellow. The earliest perennials soon follow and become colorful coverups for fading bulb foliage. Plant coral bells, periwinkle, dianthus, columbine, cushion spurge, and lady's mantle over and around spring bulbs.

repeat performance

right: **Count on this easy perennial trio to return early every summer: penstemon, cranesbill, and 'Blue Butterfly' delphinium.**

bunches of blooms
above: Blue, pink, and purple bouquets of early-spring blooms include perennial *Phlox subulata*, forget-me-not, and annual *Viola cornuta*.

tantalizing trio
left: Plumes of astilbe mingle with *Dianthus barbatus* and columbine. Lady's mantle fills in the background. These perennials thrive in partial shade and organic-enriched soil.

trios

peak season

Summer favors a red-hot color scheme that stands up and shouts despite punishing heat. Beds and borders catch fire with golden yellows, searing reds, and volcanic oranges. When composing midsummer trios, always include at least one cooldown color to keep the fire under control. A splash of silver or dabs of white take the temperature down a notch. Calming pinks and blues also moderate hot colors.

hot cha-cha

right: Annual red salvia, black-eyed Susan, and *Gaillardia* sizzle next to the cooling white of perennial Shasta daisies. Keep the daisies coming by removing faded flowers.

butterflies are free

below: Orange butterfly weed, *Aesclepias*, and yellow Asiatic lilies harmonize with spiky blue veronica. This midsummer combo attracts butterflies.

Winning three-way garden partnerships combine red, white, and yellow or orange. Orange, yellow, and blue–theme borders prove that one cool tone plus two fiery allies can hit it off. Midsummer blues come from bachelor's button, campanula, delphinium, ageratum, and ladybells. Purple, gold, and silver reflect the sun's glory in a cooler, sophisticated scheme. Imagine the refreshing and reflective nature of a shady summer oasis painted green, white, and lavender or pink.

desert dazzlers

above: Desert spoon shrub, *Dasylirion wheeleri*, fans its silvery leaves in the midst of *Verbena rigida* and *Gaillardia*. Desert natives all, the three plants form a permanent perennial planting.

endless summer

left: The orange-gold blooms of perennial *Rudbeckia* would be an overwhelming radiant mass without the interspersed cool tones of lavender aster and lamb's-ears. The bursts of sunny color continue with a little help from the pruning shears to remove faded blooms.

trios

three parts foliage

When leaves play together in three-part harmony, the garden gains textural dimensions as well as colorful special effects. The soft ripple of grasses and the whorled pinwheels of euphorbias push the gardener's brushstrokes a step further into the complexities of shape and form.

Foliage eases the way to experimenting with color. Minus flower distractions, a collage of leaves clearly shows when color combinations work. Gather leaves from the plants you'd like to include in a garden vignette and arrange them next to one another on a sheet of paper. This will give you a compass bearing to follow with your garden's design. Add flowering plants last as seasonal accents among layers of ever-fascinating foliage.

Most foliage hues mingle well. Striking burgundy or purple leaves and showy variegated foliage substitute for flowers in a leafy garden. Gold goes well with purple, and silver adds a muted sparkle to the trio. Silver, gold, and yellow-green variegated foliage compose a gorgeous blend. A landscape dominated by purple and silver foliage suggests an aura of somber mystery lightened somewhat by a chartreuse or gold highlight.

silver streak

right: **Dusty miller puts the spark into a planting of *Euphorbia wulfenii* and purple barberry. A tender annual, the dusty miller will need replacing the next season. Pluck off the flower spikes to encourage the showy foliage.**

covering ground
above: A yellow and white perennial pair, *Alyssum saxatile* 'Citrinum' and snow-in-summer, gain another dimension with fine-texture blue oat grass.

purple haze
left: The shade's aglow when purple and yellow combine, as in this team of purple heuchera, variegated green-and-gold hosta, and the golden grass, *Hakonechloa*.

portable color

container combos

Potted gardens carry color quickly and conveniently to wherever it's needed. They also furnish dress rehearsals for a future in-the-ground garden. If you're contemplating color schemes for a full-fledged bed or border, first try them out by mixing colors and textures together in a pot.

Container gardens sustain colorful plantings over a long period with some simple guidelines. Start with a pot that's large enough to accommodate plant growth and expanding root systems. Professional garden designers recommend spacious containers of at least 12 inches in diameter or larger. Plan for a dense display of color, leaving only a few inches between each plant. Always give plants as healthy a start as possible with good-quality potting soil. An organic mix that includes a high humus content and balanced fertilizers gets color off to a fast start.

box punch

above: A wooden crate spills over with Persian shield, Algerian ivy, polka-dot plant, and caladium. The tender plants can live through the winter protected indoors.

potted paradise

right: Sweet-scented heliotrope mingles with fragrant nicotiana, cascading lobelia and ivy, soft yellow-green helichrysum, and spiky New Zealand flax. Only the flax lives past summer, in Zones 6 and warmer, with protection.

twist and shout

opposite: Towering, multicolor copperleaf makes a foil for swirls of candy pink petunias and chocolate-leaf ornamental sweet potato vines. The tender tropicals offer a long-lived option for warm, humid climates.

portable color

movable feasts

Potted gardens allow unlimited freedom when it comes to choosing what plants to mix and match. Opt for anything that can live temporarily in close quarters. Annuals mix with perennials. Ornamental grasses rub elbows with small trees or bulbs.

The same color harmonies that rule beautiful permanent gardens also apply to portable ones. Cool container schemes of blues and greens project tranquillity; reds, oranges, and yellows stir things up. Pinks and lavenders integrate separate pots into a unified look. Blue contrasted with yellow, or orange with purple, puts a potted garden in the spotlight. Include varying foliage for texture and to complement or contrast. Your containers will be within close-up view, where their vivid color details can be appreciated.

color where it counts

Container plantings put color at your garden decorating beck and call, especially where ground is limited or of poor quality.

- Cluster pots of shade-loving varieties around a tree.
- Place sturdy or low-growing windproof plants on a city terrace.
- Line a path with uniform pots or planted concrete blocks.
- Group colorful containers on a fire escape.
- Flank a front door or steps with symmetrical potted shrubs or small trees.
- Hang flat-back planters on a bare wall.

Well-balanced container gardens, whether in buckets, boxes, pots, urns, or troughs, all follow the zen of an artful flower arrangement. Design begins with scale. The tallest element stands in the center or slightly off to one side. It should be two and a half times the height of the container. Medium-size plants fill in around the center; short or cascading plants on the edges complete the design.

To plant a tropical-theme container, for example, set a canna, hibiscus, or dwarf banana plant in the middle and surround it with amaranth, caladium, nicotiana, or fuchsia. Add plumbago, lantana, or ornamental sweet potato vine as the cascading grand finale.

Start a naturalistic theme with a tall grass in dramatic colors, work in a few round-profile perennials, and then shorter annuals or herbs around the rim.

ripple effect

above: **Succulents with intricately layered shapes thrive in this array of metal cauldrons and clay urns. The garden includes sempervivums and echeverias, desert natives that tolerate hot sun and dry conditions.**

plant library

left: **This vintage wooden magazine stand houses a brilliant collection of frost-tender coleus, impatiens, and verbena.**

rust bucket

opposite: **A rusty square bucket brims with an unexpected mix of houseplants and perennials, including tall *Cordyline terminalis* 'Red Sister', 'Moonbeam' coreopsis, variegated dense-flowered loosestrife *(Lysimachia)*, and the vining annual sweet potato 'Blackie'.**

potted pleasures

Container gardens please the most when they're unpredictable. Combine plants in odd numbers of three, five, or seven to achieve unexpected, asymmetrical art instead of rigid patterns. Plant summer-flowering bulbs, perennials, and new annual varieties for fun.

Use portable plantings as a visual extension of your in-ground garden. Follow the same color scheme and style to make a transition from plots to pots. Does a plain wall or a long fence in your garden beg for transformation? Decorate it with hanging baskets planted in hues that bring the background material to life. Stage potted plants on stairs or a balcony to add high notes of lushness and color.

The container itself becomes an integral element in a potted garden. In the most striking container gardens, a plant's silhouette matches that of its pot. A rounded shrub or perennial fits best in a low container that has slightly flared edges. A topiary looks its most elegant in a tall, narrow pot that suits its shape. A cascading plant makes an impression when showcased in a wide-brim urn.

Traditional shapes in plastic, terra-cotta, fiberglass, and lightweight styrene provide hospitable plant lodgings, but unexpected containers turn potted gardens into a party. Forays to garage sales, flea markets, and thrift stores may turn up that

stepping up

right: Potted plants staggered on the stairway create a brilliant transition from ground floor to deck. Tuberous begonias, geraniums, lilies, petunias, and eucomis (an elegant, summer-flowering bulb) share the stage. Support the tall lilies with an informal tripod of bamboo stakes.

chorus line

below: A hanging garden of jewel-color annuals adorns a wall with living draperies. Geraniums, petunias, nasturtiums, and bidens all have flowing shapes well suited to basket growing. Remove faded flowers to extend the summer-long show.

perfect vessel for a contained masterpiece. Buckets, wagons, wooden boxes, baskets, old chairs, and trunks offer plantable treasures. Limit your use of metal containers to shady areas, however, as metal conducts heat. Overheated plant roots cannot absorb water and will be permanently damaged. Line baskets and other containers you wish to protect with sheets of plastic stapled to the inside. Make a drainage hole or fill the bottom of the container with styrene packing material.

Found props also highlight potted gardens with whimsical touches. Miniature birdhouses on sticks, gracefully shaped branches, croquet mallets, tool heads, and other finds accessorize pots with creative color. They also make imaginative plant supports.

ultimate yard & garden | **245**

portable color: shallow bowl

zones	make it	skill
all	1 hour	easy

you will need

- one 6-inch perennial aster
- one 4-inch mum
- one 4-inch variegated ivy
- one 6-inch rock fern
- one ornamental cabbage
- one 6-inch sedum
- one 16-inch–diameter terra–cotta bowl
- scrap of window screen
- soilless potting mix

autumn display

Most container color schemes need refreshment come early fall. This easy-to-put-together potted garden celebrates fall colors with a gathering of hardy plants in tones of green, lavender, magenta, and coral. Note how the gently sloped silhouette of the plantings flatters the low, wide bowl. The circular garden is designed to look good from any angle.

Most of the bowl garden's perennial plants, including the aster, mum, and rock fern, will settle permanently in the garden if planted before the first killing frost. The sedum lives on through the winter in milder climates, such as Southern California and the Gulf Coast. Ivy overwinters indoors in climates where winter temperatures dip below freezing. The ornamental cabbage lives out its brief annual life span in the container.

If you like, substitute a plant with a comparable, overall shape and size, such as an ornamental grass instead of the aster.

bowl of fire

right: **By planting mature specimens, you'll enjoy immediate gratification from this colorful garden. Smaller plants may take longer to bloom than mature plants, but they won't outgrow a pot as quickly.**

1 organizing Starting with mature blooming plants yields a more finished look that easily lasts a month or two. Blooming plants provide color without needing long-term fertilizing and grooming. A lightweight soilless potting mix works well, as long as it is consistently watered. Note the wide diameter of the pot used for this garden. It's large enough to accommodate six plants in close quarters.

2 groundwork First, place a small, square piece of window screen over the pot's drainage hole. This will keep out sowbugs and other pests as well as prevent soil from washing out of the hole. Pour in the soilless mix halfway up to the container's rim. Dampen the mix at this point or while it's still in the bag. Arrange the plants, still in their pots, into a portrait that looks balanced and shows off each plant to its best advantage.

3 composing Slip plants out of their pots and untangle the root balls. Set each plant firmly into its permanent place, spreading the root system over the soil. Pour in more mix until the roots are covered and the container is full. Tamp down the mix around the plants to anchor them securely. Water thoroughly. Lift the planted container to a wagon or wheeled plant caddy and roll it to its display location (either in full sun or partial shade).

ultimate yard & garden | **247**

portable color: tips

1   **root check** Root-bound plants have become dry and thirsty before you even bring them home. Once planted, they won't perform to potential. Avoid purchasing root-bound plant material; choose alternative plants. Inspect the drainage holes in larger potted plants for protruding roots, which indicate the plant has outgrown its pot. Slide smaller plants from their packs and check for tangled root balls.

As you plant container gardens, prime the plants' root systems for new growth by teasing or breaking open the root balls and spreading the roots out gently. Water potted plants before transplanting for easier removal from their original nursery containers. When starting with bare-root plants, keep them in a plastic bag and moisten regularly until planting.

2   **take a load off** Save on planting time, potting soil, and backaches with a few tricks tucked inside your chosen container. A small plastic nursery pot, inverted and propped on the bottom, takes up space that would otherwise be filled with soil, making the container easier to lift and carry. Fill the remainder of the pot with soil, leaving room for plants. Alternatively, recycle styrene packing material by using it as a filler for the bottom third of large containers. Also, use a decorative container, especially one without a drainage hole, as a cachepot for one or more plants in ordinary plastic nursery pots. The double layer insulates plants from heat and moisture evaporation.

3

4

change of seasons When the **3** summer celebrities of your container garden fade at season's end, have some cool-season stand-ins ready. Fresh plant material keeps the garden's color going until frost. Mums, ornamental cabbages and kale, ornamental grasses, asters, fall crocus, pansies, dianthus, and snapdragons respond with vigor to the cool kiss of fall mornings. In the photo at left, asters, mums, and cape fuchsia take center stage for the fall color rally.

colorful colonies Container **4** plants love company. Aesthetically, grouped containers have a much stronger impact than a lone potted plant. Garden designers recommend staging pots together in odd-number populations. Make one large container the focus of a potted garden, then encircle it with a supporting cast of smaller pots. A group of pots clustered together also creates a microclimate that protects the plant population from wind and heat. The shadows of surrounding pots shade root zones and keep them cool, promoting healthy growth during summer heat. Before you leave for vacation, crowd your containers together and water them thoroughly; they'll keep one another shaded and cool for several days.

For help visualizing what your garden might look like when you add elements, go to the interactive garden design tool at **www.bhg.com/bkplanagarden**

inspirational gardens

early-season gardens 252
midseason gardens 254
late-season gardens 258
harvest-season gardens 262
multiseason garden 266
extending color 270
lasting color 276
artists' gardens 282
 oregon 282
 iowa 284
 british columbia 286
 missouri 288
 california 290

early-season gardens

spring portrait

Spring at first sight: a faint chartreuse haze veils the bare branches of winter. Suddenly, shooting stars and trilliums appear. The lawn hosts a brief showing of wild violets. Fruit tree blossoms paint the horizon with white clouds. Daffodil rivers run under trees. In California and the Southwest, flocks of poppies and lupines mark the end of the rainy season.

The palette expands by the week. Parades of lollipop-hue tulips march through gardens, and forsythias bear flowers of school-bus yellow. The soft pinks, whites, and lavenders of lilacs and peonies soon follow, trailing sweet perfumes.

Colors come and go quickly in this briefest of seasons, so plan for early-, mid-, and late-spring color. Wrap the brilliant blooms of bulbs in envelopes of flowering shrubs.

on the wall color

above: **Tulips are the undoubted stars in this rock wall scene, but more long-lasting color comes from pansies, candytuft, and gold-tint shrubs.**

post-chill thrills

opposite: **A welcome sight after a cold winter, forsythia and lively crowds of tulips require extended cold to bloom their best.**

great plants for early-season gardens

arabis

bleeding heart, page 112

candytuft, page 116

columbine, page 107

crocus

cushion spurge, page 114

daffodil

dianthus, page 112

forget-me-not

forsythia

grape hyacinth

Greek windflower, page 107

hellebore, page 115

iris, pages 130–131

jack-in-the-pulpit

lilac

lily-of-the-valley, page 111

oriental poppy, page 120

pansy

peony, page 119

pulmonaria, page 121

redbud

rhododendron

snowdrop

soapwort, page 122

tulip

viola

wake-robin, page 125

wallflower

white forsythia

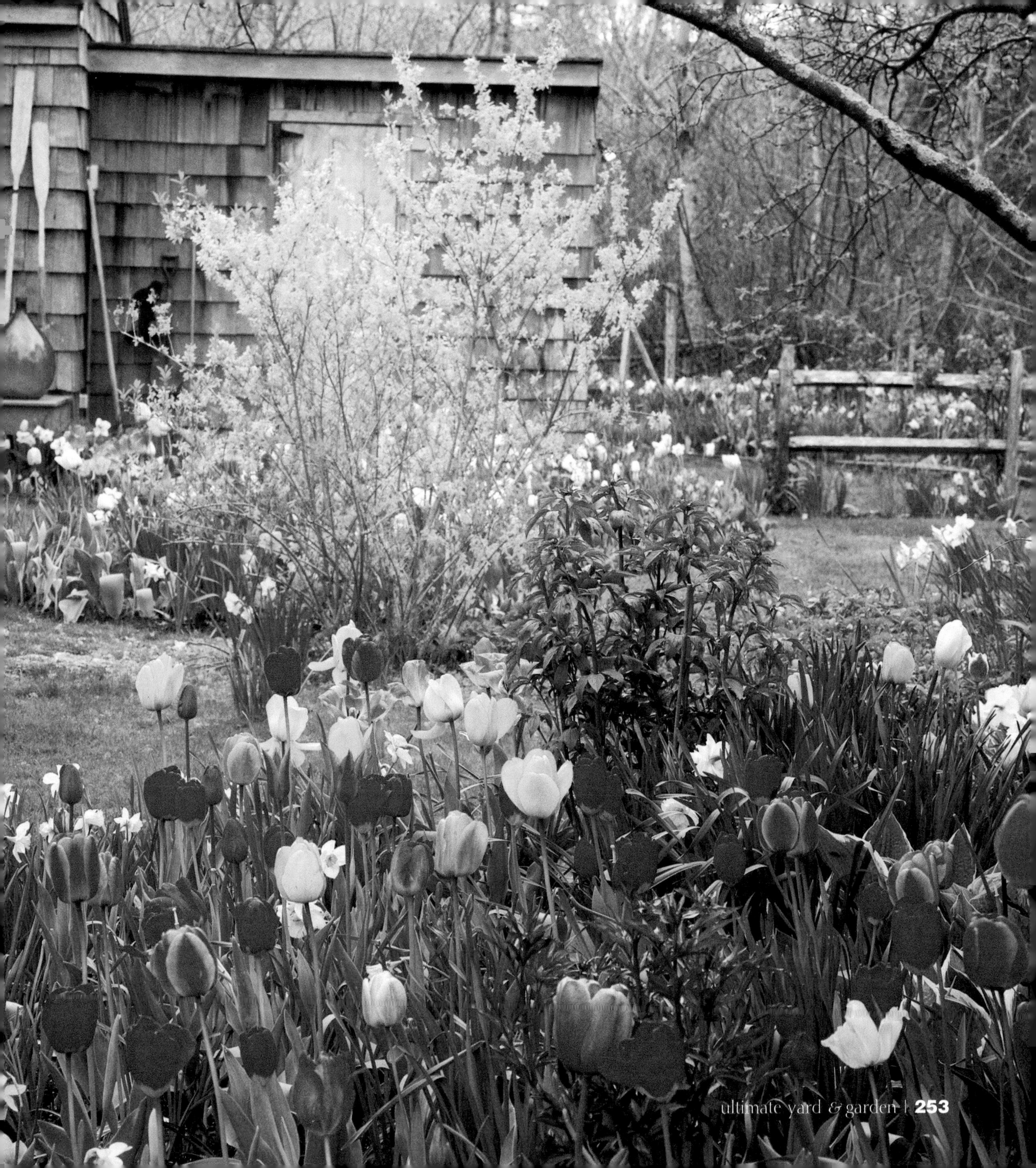

midseason gardens

the curtain rises

Summer's first long days quicken the pace of plant growth and flowering. Traditional blooms, such as roses and delphiniums, begin unfurling to their season in the sun. Tropical cannas, callas, New Zealand flaxes, and fuchsias soar into action after the last frost date. Heat-worshipping annuals, including cosmos, zinnias, petunias, and sunflowers, keep company with perennial black-eyed Susans, lilies, coreopsis, and ornamental grasses.

The warm season brings its own challenge: How do you keep color waves breaking with no doldrums in between? Plan ahead.

cool summer shrine

right: 'Johnson's Blue' geranium, 'Elijah' blue fescue, 'Betty Prior' rose, and roly-poly alliums transform a plain urn and gray fountain into artwork. The soft color scheme also coordinates with the white house.

tropical fantasia

opposite: Romantic summer landscaping involves yellow canna, coneflowers, *Phygelius*, and New Zealand flax paired with the more traditional white lily and hydrangea.

great plants for midseason gardens

baby's breath, page 114	delphinium, page 112
bellflower, page 110	fuchsia
black-eyed susan, page 122	hydrangea
calendula	lavender, page 122
canna	lily, page 117
cardinal flower, page 118	ornamental grass, pages 128–129
cleome	rose
cosmos	salvia, page 122
daylily	speedwell, page 125

midseason gardens

peak summer

Look to a succession of annuals in late spring and summer to fill gaps between perennials and to echo perennial color schemes.

Backdrops of single shrubs or trees that exhibit an interesting feature, such as colored foliage, berries, or textured bark, also anchor the summer garden while temporary color drifts arrive, and then melt away. Green shrubbery, such as herbs and boxwood, forms a frame that buffers bright, hot flower colors and knits the color scheme into an integrated vision.

Shape your summer border's core with perennials selected for spice whether in or out of bloom. Consider form and foliage beyond bloom color. Spiky perennials teamed up with mounded plants and gold leaves paired with multihue ones lend a sense of continuity during the season's hustle and bustle. Also, choose one dependable element, such as a hedge of ever-blooming roses or an herb-lined path in a linking color, and use it to join your garden's color blocks.

plant list

1 'six hills giant' catmint, page 119

2 borage

3 bellflower, page 110

4 lavender, page 122

5 'the pearl' yarrow, page 106

6 dwarf boxwood

7 golden oregano

8 orris, pages 130–131

balancing act

left and *opposite:* The use of potted boxwoods, raised-bed frames, and architectural foliage (irises and alliums) introduces classical elements into a tousled flower and herb garden. Carefree perennials (catmint and yarrow) mingle with reseeding annuals (calendula and California poppies). In cold-winter climates, keep the potted boxwoods in a cool, sheltered place, such as a garage or sunporch, during the cold months.

late-season gardens

dazzling dog days

In late summer, heat-struck gardens often turn as sullen as the air just before a thunderstorm. Prevent garden color fatigue by planting long-blooming varieties. Use daylilies, such as 'Stella de Oro' or 'Bitsy', to brighten up a sunny border for several weeks.

Involve late-flowering perennials, including *Conoclinium coelestinum*, boltonia, aconite, Japanese anemone, and goldenrod, in your plan. They'll pick up color-theme threads where earlier-blooming perennials leave off. Plant several species within a plant group to enjoy a long-playing show. Asiatic, Oriental, and Regal (Trumpet) lilies provide varying bloom times and explosions of color.

bright lights
above right: **'Enchantment' Asiatic lilies, baby's breath, Shasta daisies, and 'Bonica' roses offer a rare late-summer freshness.**

lily allure
right: **Fragrant *Lilium regale* and daylilies have late- and long-blooming tendencies.**

late show
opposite: **A late-season flowering paradise is possible in this Zone 5 garden because it includes marathon bloomers and late varieties.**

late-season gardens

ripened color

Late-season gardens offer a perfect opportunity to show off plants in their second prime. Many annuals and perennials have richly colored and textured ornamental seedpods. Pearly disks of lunaria flutter in the breeze. Cardoon and teasel seed heads resemble intricately woven baskets. Allium flower heads imitate miniature satellites.

Rose species that develop large hips will start doing so now if faded blooms aren't removed. Viburnum, pyracantha, hawthorn, and dogwood become laden with berries. Besides the rich patina they add to garden palettes, plants allowed to go to seed also make your yard a destination favored by wildlife, especially migratory birds.

great plants for late-season gardens

amaranth	feverfew, page 124
astilbe (late-blooming), page 108	goldenrod, page 123
	japanese anemone
baby's breath, page 114	joe-pye weed, page 113
celosia	lunaria
coreopsis 'moonbeam', page 111	mistflower
daylily 'stella de oro', page 115	regal lily
	rose
delphinium, page 112	salvia, page 122
echinacea	shasta daisy

go wild

right: **Fall migratory birds will flock to this free-for-all corner of a harvest garden. The colorful smorgasbord of sunflower, goldenrod,** *Lunaria,* **amaranth, and coneflower pleases the eye and bird palates too.**

A few perennials rebloom as days grow shorter, after first flowering in early summer. Some bearded iris varieties, delphinium, and clematis share this remontant (reblooming) timing. Additional perennials prolong their colorful performance if sheared back after a midsummer flowering. This list includes black-eyed Susan, coreopsis, and helenium. Chrysanthemums produce large late-season flowers if buds are removed until midsummer.

With minimal nurturing and maximum planning, the summer garden sustains the show through its very last curtain call. A top layer of compost applied in fall and spring, plus a sprinkling of slow-release fertilizer or organic nutrients early in the season, ensures that summer's promise comes true.

big picture
above left: Layers of ornamental grasses, dahlias, and chrysanthemums compose a blazing fall scenario. Dig dahlias' tuberous roots and store them indoors over winter in cold climates.

summer meets fall
left: Tender Mexican sage *(Salvia leucantha),* lamb's-ears, and a flurry of white Japanese anemone flowers stand up to the brilliant fall colors of chrysanthemums.

ultimate yard & garden | **261**

harvest-season gardens

gilded fall gardens

In fall, more so than any other season, brilliant pigments come from sources other than flowers. Changing foliage of trees and shrubs, ripened seed heads, and bronzed ornamental grasses all share in creating the richest of the seasonal palettes.

Ornamental grasses endow the autumnal garden with a slightly untamed look. Imposing and rhythmic in the wind, they deepen dramatically in color as temperatures drop and days shorten. Combined with perennials that bloom late, including *Rudbeckia, Sedum spectabile,* Russian sage, aster, and mum, grasses add delicate texture to the fall garden. They project a sense of haunting wistfulness at the blooming season's end. Their show will go on, however, extending architecture and rare color into the winter garden. For that reason, as well as the cover and seeds they offer wildlife, delay trimming grasses until early spring.

autumn rainbows

above right: **There's plenty of flower power left in this fall border of** *Polygonum* **'Firetail',** *Echinacea* **'White Swan', astilbe, and shrubby** *Caryopteris.* **These perennials will continue to provide food and shelter for overwintering wildlife, so spring is the best time to prune.**

roadside attractions

right: **A brilliant-color cornucopia of fall blooms, including aster, dahlia, sunflower, ornamental oregano, and lamb's-ear, attracts human and winged visitors for exploration.**

enter fall

opposite: **A magnificent, undisciplined planting mixes late-blooming perennials such as globe thistle, coneflower, butterfly bush, and ornamental grasses with sweet potato vine. The warm fall color scheme reflects the home's facade.**

harvest-season gardens

reaping riches

Fall glory realizes the best-laid plans made
in spring. Trees and shrubs planted then pay
dividends in spectacular fall foliage. Oaks, birches,
beeches, dogwoods, maples (Japanese maples,
in particular), ginkgos, persimmons, and sweet
gums show their autumnal colors with
the cooler weather.

Many perennials also show reddened or
gilded leaves at the first touch of frost. Those
with changing fall color include epimedium, peony,
gaura, *Geranium psilostemon*, and some euphorbias.
Shrubs such as euonymus, oakleaf hydrangea,
aronia, sumac, viburnum, and blueberry also
catch fire in the fall, as do grapes, Virginia creeper,
Boston ivy, and other vines.

The blooming continues in the autumn garden
as dahlia, Joe-pye weed, mistflower (*Conoclinium*

autumn jewels
above right: The
fiery plumes of late-
flowering annual
celosia pair with
perennial *Rudbeckia*,
milkweed, ornamental
grass, fern, and
thinleaf zinnia.
It's a border scheme
that birds will seek
out for seeds.

metallic magic
right: Japanese
maples flame with
fall color. Perennial
Epimedium,
Rodgersia, fern, and
hellebore skirt the
maples with copper,
bronze, and scarlet.

coelestinum), milkweed, and aconite display their finest flower color. Many blooms attract butterflies in their fall migration. Autumn-flowering clematis (*C. ternifolia* 'Sweet Autumn') wafts a sweet scent and enhances fall's textural collage with its fluffy seed heads. Warm-weather annuals, including zinnia, celosia, globe amaranth, and castor bean, continue blooming vigorously until the first frost. Gardeners in warm regions can also find unusual sources of fall color in the bronze and purple leaves of tropical cannas and bananas, plus a variety of brilliant-color houseplants.

Harvest now to bring the garden's color indoors with arrangements of dried flowers and seed heads. Also collect ripened seeds to regenerate your garden "paints" for the next year's palette.

great plants for harvest-season gardens

aster, page 108	milkweed
black-eyed susan, page 122	mistflower
broom corn	ornamental grasses, pages 128–129
canna	ornamental kale
chrysanthemum, page 111	pansy
clematis ternifolia, page 111	russian sage, page 120
globe thistle	sedum 'autumn joy', page 123
japanese maple	spicebush
knot weed	sumac

brazen duo

left: **Who would have thought that North American native Joe-pye weed and tropical bronze-leaf canna would hit it off so well? Both tall plants benefit from moist soil. Store tender canna roots indoors over the winter.**

multiseason garden

altered states

The same garden wears three different costumes that change with the season. Spring's color plan shifts easily into summer's with no lag if executed by planning ahead.

Hardy annuals such as godetia, dianthus, candytuft, stock, sweet alyssum, and pansy go into the ground before spring's last frost, which they can survive. Their color progresses into early summer. Meanwhile, more tender summer annuals get an inconspicuous green start, hidden behind the spring blooms.

As summer blooms wane and mums replace them, ornamental grasses and asters come to the fore, dominating the landscape with broad sweeps of texture.

spring pink

above right: The cottage gets a lift from a pink-theme tulip bed rimmed in grape hyacinths.

summer yellow

right: Snapdragons and marigolds replace tulips, filling in among perennial *Rudbeckias*.

fall gold

opposite: Maiden grass and fountain grass round out the fall palette, along with lavender aster and bronze mum.

multiseason garden

color transition tips

Spend the bulk of your color budget on prominent areas. Keep the color fresh and ever changing in those places, such as the front door or along a well-trod path. Focus on generous plantings around hardscape features, including rock outcroppings, arbors, walkways, fountains, and other destinations where people will enter or linger awhile.

Make seasonal transitions colorful and effortless with these strategies: Start planning for the next

transient spring

right: **Spring bulbs, including grape hyacinths, anemones, and tulips, pop up amid hardy annuals planted early in the season. 'Goldflame' spirea across the bridge and newly emerged sedum provide perennial landmarks.**

great plants for multiseason gardens

early–season	delphinium, page 112
anemone	impatiens
candytuft, page 116	scabiosa
creeping phlox	twinspur
grape hyacinth	veronica
hellebore, page 115	**late–season**
silene	aster, page 108
spirea 'goldflame'	black-eyed susan, page 122
sweet pea	
tulip	chrysanthemum, page 111
vinca	marigold
midseason	sedum, page 123
bergenia, page 109	toad lily
chamomile, page 110	verbena
coneflower, page 122	

season before it starts. Create space by removing whatever's tired or underperforming. Treat spring tulips as annuals, planting them thickly the previous fall, then lifting them before the foliage fades. Dig up faded summer annuals and plug in mums at summer's end.

Refresh summer borders by pruning and roguing tired plants. Keep an out-of-the-way nursery bed planted with leftover pack plants, immature perennials, or extra annuals you've started from seed. These will supply your borders with fresh-face reinforcements as summer marches on. Overwinter any leftover perennials in the nursery and transplant them into the garden the following year.

Pack window boxes and other containers densely with plants big enough for instant impact. As portable gardens, potted plants earn their keep in high-exposure areas.

When planting late-season borders, select quart- or gallon-size perennials. The plants flower the first year and grow large enough to divide their second season, thus returning your initial investment. Ornamental grasses also represent money well spent, because they make colorful contributions in three seasons, not just one. Plant bulbs in fall plus early annuals in spring to camouflage stubs of trimmed grasses.

short summer
above left: A footbridge with a rock garden in the foreground serves as a focal point year-round. Salmon impatiens, blue veronica, and 'Lulu' marigold brighten the edges.

extended fall
left: Perennial sedums and sedges, combined with freshly planted mums, adorn the bridge garden with fall highlights. The mums fill gaps left behind by spent summer annuals.

extending color

shortcuts to success

Propagating plants by division gives your garden
broad brushstrokes of color in a short time. Once
mature, perennial plants yield several divisions,
allowing you to repeat the color groupings
throughout your borders. Take the fastest route
by starting your garden with larger plants in
one-gallon pots. They'll be ready to divide within
a year or two.

Divide root balls of perennials either in
spring or fall, depending on plant bloom times.
Large-leaf, unwieldy plants, such as hostas,
ornamental grasses, and daylilies, divide more
easily if dug in early spring when the plants
emerge. Divide and replant lilies-of-the-valley,
Shasta daisies, hellebores, astilbes, and other
early-spring-flowering perennials in fall.

multiplied by root division

astilbe, page 108	oregano
coreopsis, page 111	ornamental grasses, pages 128-129
daylily, page 115	
ferns, page 126-127	peony, page 119
gaura	phlox, page 120
hellebore, page 115	salvia, page 122
hosta, page 116	sedum, page 123
iris	shasta daisy
lily-of-the-valley, page 111	thyme, page 124
	vinca

divide to multiply

right: 'Moonbeam' coreopsis, 'Elijah' blue
fescue, 'Autumn Joy' sedum, lavender, purple
coneflower, and Russian sage are just a few
of the many perennials that respond well to
root division.

1 dig In fall, trim back a perennial before dividing the plant. (Less bulk on top makes divisions easier to pull apart.) Then insert a sharp-edge spade or pitchfork and dig around the plant's circumference. Dig around the plant again to completely dislodge it. Use the spade or fork under the plant to help lift it. Plants lift more easily in dry weather when you water them thoroughly the day you plan to divide them.

2 lift out Lift the plant, including the root ball and attached soil, from the garden. If the plant doesn't move easily, reinsert the shovel to detach any clinging roots. Squat and use your leg muscles to lift the plant and avoid back injury. Place the plant on nearby ground. Trim back the tops of thickly thatched perennials such as ornamental grasses, bamboos, and coreopsis. It will make the dividing easier to accomplish.

3 divide Although this process is called root division, it actually separates parts of the plant crown with roots attached. Use your hands to push the plant stems to either side, locating a natural part in the crown. Then use a sharp-edge spade to divide the plant in half. Divide the halves into additional sections, if you like. Replant the divisions and water thoroughly.

changeable hydrangeas

A constant source of summer garden color comes from the billowy blooms of hydrangeas. Stalwart shrubs for shade, they live for years and display handsome foliage when their bloom period is past. Several hydrangea hybrids, plus a handful of species, are available by mail order, or check with your local garden center's shrub department. Plant a variety of hydrangeas to have color waves from early summer to fall and fresh or dried flowers indoors.

Many varieties of *Hydrangea macrophylla* (bigleaf or mophead and lacecap) respond to soil pH. In acidic soil, plants produce spectacular blue blooms. Alkaline to neutral soils yield rosy pink flowers that age to magenta. Treat garden soil to alter bloom color by adding iron sulfate or elemental sulfur to acidify or hydrated lime or superphosphate to boost alkalinity. Two basics to remember: Know your soil's pH before you start and apply soil amendments before flower buds appear. It may take several months for a color change to develop. Some white-flowering types and some new varieties retain their color regardless of the soil pH.

Crisp white blooms of the peegee hydrangea and towering snow cones of oakleaf hydrangea offer summer refreshment too, especially in partially shaded sites. A color bonus: the foliage of these species reddens in fall.

flaunt those big blues

right: Cool lavender-blue mophead hydrangeas create a welcoming oasis for relaxing in the garden. A naturally acidic soil enhances the color. Boost soil acidity by adding iron sulfate or elemental sulfur (¼ cup dissolved in a gallon of water).

hydrangea alchemy

left: Some pink hydrangea varieties shift color from green to cream, deepen to pink, and then age to magenta. To help cut hydrangeas stay fresh longer, crush stem ends with a hammer before placing them in water.

lasting pleasure

below: Harvest hydrangea blooms in late summer or early fall and dry them for months of enjoyment indoors. Let flowers air dry in a vase without water.

extending color

comeback color

Timely plant manicures thwart plants' natural goal of seed setting, thus guaranteeing a continuous supply of flower color. Any plant that belongs to the composite or daisy family, especially, benefits from occasional flower snipping. This includes zinnia, coreopsis, aster, boltonia, marguerite, helenium, and other summer garden stars.

Stimulate bloom by feeding perennials with a low-nitrogen, high-phosphorus fertilizer (5-10-5); give annuals a balanced (10-10-10) formula.

snip and grow

right: Dense-flowering zinnias run a constant race toward seed setting to ensure future generations. The more faded flower heads are removed, the more new blooms form.

rose grooming

below: Long-blooming roses, such as 'Sally Holmes' and 'Joseph's Coat', continue their color show all summer. Stimulate flowering by cutting just-open blooms for vase life or snipping spent blooms.

mulch A coat of insulating mulch protects plant crowns from winter freeze-and-thaw cycles, and it keeps plant roots cooler in summer and preserves soil moisture. Consistent moisture keeps flowers fresh and longer lasting. Mulch summer flower borders and shrubs with 1 to 2 inches of organic material, including chopped leaves, shredded bark, cocoa bean hulls, or compost.

snap off Showcase daylily flowers and other plants that develop several blooms per stalk in a manner they deserve by snapping off blooms past their prime. Lilies, gladiolas, crocosmias, hollyhocks, and irises all benefit from this action. Pull down gently on the withered flower until it snaps off cleanly.

snip Signal the next wave of blooms to form by clipping off stems of withered flowers. Snipping rejuvenates all types of flowers that grow in spikes, such as delphinium, veronica, salvia, and foxglove, as well as yarrow, rose, and daisy types. Use hand pruners or sharp scissors to deadhead flowers on fibrous stems. Cut off the faded flowers about ¼ inch above the next bud. Snipping encourages new blooms on coneflowers, coreopsis, hostas, and zinnias.

pinch Crops of maximum-size flowers reward the gardener who disbuds plants such as mums, dahlias, carnations, and peonies. Disbudding diverts the flow of growth hormones, food, and water from many to a few stems and remaining buds. Pinch off all but the main bud on a stem.

lasting color

lingering looks

The longest-lasting color comes from permanent garden features. When researching garden candidates, keep your region's climate in mind. Plants that melt with mildew won't endure hot and humid Southeast summers. Mountain gardeners want annuals that tolerate warm days and cool nights with equal aplomb, getting off to a fast start equal to the short growing season. Southwest gardeners need plants that flourish in dry summers. Plants native to your region or to similar climates have the best potential. Search out hybrids developed from these well-adapted plants.

top 10 perennials for lasting color

baby's breath, page 114	gaillardia
campanula (dwarf)	scabiosa
coreopsis, page 111	speedwell, page 125
cranesbill, page 114	valerian
evening primrose	yarrow, page 106

don juan and friends

above right: Ordinary lattice becomes a wall of color when it supports a long-blooming 'Don Juan' rose. Tender tropicals, including coleus, impatiens, and ornamental sweet potato vine, bask in the shade of the rosy canopy.

annual showstopper

right: 'Mr. Wonderful' coleus dazzles all season without fuss.

spicy border

opposite: Orange marigolds and variegated sage punch up the color quotient in a garden where bright pots provide portable color.

lasting color

marathon blooms

Color plays a significant role in flower breeding. Because fashion and decorating color trends shift so rapidly, however, seed companies focus more on long-range patterns, including consumer interest in unusual flower colors and variegated leaves.

Breeders also select flowers with long-lasting colors. Among pansies, a blue-flowering variety usually opens first and lasts longest, possibly because its wild viola ancestors all originally had blue flowers. Yellow, orange, and red flowers hold up best when exposed to strong sun, so these shades receive attention in new bedding plant varieties, especially for hotter climates. Early bloomers get special focus from bedding plant breeders because of an emphasis on pack plants that will show strong color while sitting on garden-center shelves.

cascading color

right: **Nierembergia, heliotrope, and golden dahlberg daisy keep the color waves rolling when faded flowers are sheared off. Pools of silver artemisia enhance the hot colors.**

cool corner

below: **Lobelia and pansy flowers glow against concrete edging. Deadheading flowers prompts rebloom.**

lissie who?

left: In the wild, the satiny flowers and blue-gray leaves of lisianthus have evolved to deflect heat and survive hot, arid conditions. Flower breeders have developed hybrids for long-lived cut flowers and drought-tolerant bedding plants.

summer parasols

below: Cosmos produce multitudes of silky petals in pink, magenta, white, yellow, and orange. This summer annual grows from scattered seed. Clip off spent flowers weekly. Harvest seeds at the season's end for next year.

top 10 annuals for lasting color

cleome	marigold
cosmos	nasturtium
geranium	nierembergia
impatiens	portulaca
lisianthus	sweet pea

lasting color

hardy breeds

Certain flowers come with a long-term color warranty. Their durability relates to petal thickness and how tightly the blossoms hold to the plant, as well as the plant's relative hardiness.

Perennials that flower the longest include blue flax, catmint (*Nepeta*), campanula, aster, scabiosa, veronica, spiderwort, fringed bleeding heart, evening primrose, and phlox. It's no accident of breeding that most of these are native North American plants. For an extensive list of plants searchable by name, type, and even bloom color, go to **ww.bhg.com/bkplantindex**

Not all garden color trends prove lasting. That collection of green flowers you had to have last year may not suit your fancy next year. Keep in mind that your garden evolves with your tastes, so go ahead and plant a bed of your current favorite flowers and enjoy.

prairie palette

above right: Perennial coneflowers and black-eyed Susans hail from the prairie, where their flowers cheerfully endure intense heat.

sunny spotlight

right: A concrete birdbath becomes the center of attention when surrounded by flattering hues of 'Early Sunrise' coreopsis, 'Heritage' rose, *Campanula carpatica*, 'Goldflame' spirea, and spiderwort.

hummer haven

left: Bee balm, annual red salvia, nicotiana, and 'Blue Butterfly' dwarf delphinium attract hummingbirds. Many flowers with prolonged color supply nectar for hummers throughout the summer.

hot and hotter

below: Two perennials prized for long-lasting blooms, coreopsis and daylily, warm summer borders with an array of sizzling golds, oranges, and reds. Snap off faded daylily blooms to encourage healthy plants. Deadhead coreopsis and a wave of new blooms will appear.

ultimate yard & garden | **281**

artists' gardens: oregon

This Pacific Northwest watercolorist tints her one-acre masterpiece in Portland with the same vibrant hues as her paintings. Each of the garden's six rooms reflects her talent for harmonizing plant textures and hardscape elements. Pottery, stone benches, and paving work cohesively with color themes. Half the garden is shady, so the garden artist plants layers of intriguing foliage in textural contrasts. Sun lovers, including her favorite daylily, take center stage in the exposed front-yard border. Flowering shrubs complete the plant palette.

chris keylock williams

In gardening, as well as in art, patience and the creative process bring unexpected results. "The things that go wrong lead me to try something new that turns out to be even more successful than I had hoped. I paint a background a different color and the flowers suddenly pop out. That happens in the garden too. I struggle with certain plants and have to give up and go on to some other idea. I let the design evolve."

mellow ambience
Gold-and-green
variegated holly provides
a flattering backdrop for
the yellow *Brugmansia*
in a rustic urn. The
overall effect is protected
and intimate.

light and dark
A crazy quilt of textures
makes this shady bed pop
visually. Starry-flower
campanula, hydrangea,
hosta, Australian violet,
and a seasonal focus of
impatiens mix it up under
a flowering plum tree.

sun catchers
A sunny border of daylily
celebrities shines brighter
when complemented with
the gray lace foliage and
gold button blooms of
curry plant. 'Helaman',
an orange-rim daylily,
stands in the foreground.
A fawn-color flagstone
path meandering through
the borders harmonizes
with the warm-color
flower palette.

lessons from the gardener

- Bright-hue daylilies look more color saturated when combined with silvery foliage, including curry plant and artemisia, or fine-texture plants such as feverfew.
- Compose garden scenes by highlighting flowers and foliage with objects, such as pottery, a bench, or a birdbath.
- Where shade prevails, contrast broad sweeps of dark and light colors in your garden paintings.
- Juxtapose prominent hosta foliage with the delicate blades of gold or lime green carex grass. Carex, or sedge, enjoys the same moist conditions as hostas.

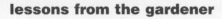

artists' gardens: iowa

The rolling rural landscape boasts a gem of a garden that includes only the hardiest plants. Its artist specializes in composing vignettes that bring out the colorful personalities of perennials. All can stand up to the rigors of Midwest weather with minimal tending. The garden's island beds spill over with free-form portraits of perennials displaying their best potential.

karen strohbeen

The first priority in the art of combining perennials: "Mostly you should please yourself," says Karen. To compose a botanical painting, she suggests a stroll through your yard to gather materials. Place flowers and foliage in a vase and arrange them into a portrait you find attractive. That's how to approach garden designing, as well. Be open to possibilities; take chances, Karen advises. Plant some personality or whimsy in your garden.

lessons from the gardener

- Use gray foliage as a color enhancer, especially with pastel colors. Any flower color looks stronger when standing next to gray.
- Plant densely in superb soil that is well amended with compost and peat moss. Set plants roughly 25 percent closer than their labels suggest. This creates a living mulch that crowds out weeds and reduces maintenance.
- Train a clematis to climb through an evergreen by planting the vine about a foot away from the tree trunk and gently tying it to the boughs until the vine wends its own way.

Clockwise, from top left:

connecting dots
A 'Betty Prior' rose shines against the fuzzy texture of a dwarf baby's breath *(Gypsophila paniculata* 'Compacta')* and blue *Allium caeruleum*.

nurture nature
Karen starts new plants in nursery beds and learns about their growth habits, bloom time, compatibility, and disease problems before moving them into the garden.

carefree combo
Blue *Clematis × durandii* contrasts in color and shape with the flat flower heads of golden 'Moonshine' yarrow and dots of *Allium caeruleum*.

spring sunrise
Newly emerged mounds of green-and-gold perennial foliage highlight the variegated leaves of *Iris pallida* 'Aureo-variegata' and the blue spikes of grape hyacinth.

peaks and valleys
A purple tower of *Clematis × iackmanii* accents a bed of 'Bitsy' daylily, *Iris spuria*, and golden barberry. Dwarf evergreen trees round out the scene.

This urban living art gallery was planted with a

jackhammer. *An asphalt driveway has given way to drifts of flower and leaf artistry that reflect the region's constantly changing light. Within sedate arborvitae walls, the plantings showcase a richly painted house in a nine-color coat of terra-cotta to teal. Bowling balls, urns, and other art pieces punctuate the rippling curves of borders and an extensive container garden. Art takes shape everywhere, with a sense of humor and fun.*

lessons from the gardener

- Direct the eye within your garden compositions: Echo the same plant repeatedly in a diagonal pattern.
- Instead of planting solid blocks of color, take a more subtle, naturalistic approach. Repeat a plant farther back in the border to create a sense of depth and a self-sown look.
- Artful elements such as colorful bowling balls and vintage chairs, when well placed, fuse garden beds into exuberant configurations.
- When trees and shrubs reach full leaf during the growing season, mark where you plan to create arches and openings with late-winter pruning.

Clockwise, from top left:

gallery showing

A potted garden gathers around an artful table and a bowling ball. *Clematis × jackmanii* sprawls out to form a purple backdrop.

bowling ball chic

A bowling ball poised in an Art Deco stand echoes the coppery color of bladder senna, or *Colutea,* flowers dangling from above.

electric eclectic

Potted salvia, New Zealand flax, and assorted succulents set off the painted terra-cotta and teal house exterior. These plants thrive in the hot, dry conditions created by sun reflecting off concrete.

valerie murray

The art of gardening entails relating smaller groups to the larger overall picture through echoes and transitions, says Valerie. But a garden is not like a painting that "needs to be hung and demands to be looked at. You can't hang onto it, you have to be in the moment. It is about process, like music, and when the light changes, everything changes."

On the edge of the woods and prairie, the possibilities of single colors play out when massed in individual beds. The paintbox garden encircles a stucco garden shed centerpiece. Each corner of the romantic spread curves into transitional areas that lead to an orchard, a vegetable garden, an arbor, and a woodland border. Enriched soil keeps the color flowing.

ouida touchón

"Monet liked masses of color, and he painted the garden with blooming plants. I attempt to do the same thing in a much smaller space … . I think of garden design as an art form. When I'm planting, I am considering color and bloom time, but I'm also considering the way the forms of one plant will work with the forms and shapes of the other plants. I look at it in a three-dimensional way."

Clockwise, from opposite top:

spring things

In Ouida's pink garden, 'Imperial Pink' pansies contribute a whole spectrum of watercolor-tinted petals, from rosy to deep plum, through the spring. She snaps off faded flowers to prolong the annual pansy's life in the garden and continue its color parade.

garden blues

Ouida holds a watercolor inspired by her blue garden, which is visible in the background.

beyond greens

The bronze and deep green of 'Rouge d'Hiver' lettuce leaves sparkle in the sun and capture the artistic gardener's attention. Lettuce makes a brilliant edging plant for flower beds as well as vegetable plots.

room with a view

A stucco garden shed (not shown) overlooks the blue garden, where ageratum, globe thistle, salvia, butterfly bush, and forget-me-not share their misty blue hues among drifts of silvery lamb's-ears and dusty miller. *Tuteurs* in the far corners support roses, while an urn captivates from the center of the formal design.

lessons from the gardener

- A formal design, featuring a series of separate beds, facilitates organization of plantings devoted to single colors, such as yellow, orange, red, pink, purple, and blue.
- Weave potted annuals into a perennial border to provide substitute color during lapses in blooms.
- Develop transitional areas, including curved paths and arbors, to link formal and casual garden plantings.
- A repetitive edging, such as dianthus or santolina, gives the most eclectic or sprawling garden a cohesive look.
- Possibilities for a blue garden include ageratum, globe thistle, 'Sky Beauty' Dutch iris, 'Victoria' salvia, anchusa, brunnera, butterfly bush, allium, sea holly, borage, blue lobelia, and forget-me-not.

ultimate yard & garden | **289**

artists' gardens: california

A floating feather, a tiny cucumber, jewel-like berries, and other garden minutiae fuel this artist's imagination. On a tree-sheltered hillside above the sea, the garden has a natural beauty that prompts sketches of bugs and blossoms. Well-nurtured vegetable and cutting plots flourish. Rugged, time-tested plants survive grazing deer. Birds find a paradise of food and shelter here.

lessons from the gardener

- Plant bearded iris, crocosmia, camellias, rhododendrons, Texas privet, and herbs, such as lavender and lemon balm, for hardy color additions that won't tempt deer.
- Provide water in protected spaces to entice birds into the garden.
- Old broken-down ladders have a second life in the garden as props for fast-growing vines.
- Interplant flowers, herbs, fruits, and vegetables for a richly diverse garden.
- Organically grown vegetable gardens produce high yields using the intensive method: deeply dug soil enriched with compost and leaf mold, carefully spaced plantings, and raised beds.

maryjo koch

Gardeners experience an intimacy with nature every day, Maryjo observes. They become artists of sorts the minute their hands touch soil. "When you're gardening, you're really observing and getting into it, just like when you're painting. You're touching the soil and feeling the soil and getting your hands into it. You're distinguishing certain smells: The smells of the soil, the smell after it rains, the fragrance of all the flowers. Those details become a part of you, just as when you paint."

Clockwise, from above:
fresh–air studio
A weathered bench, warmed by the sun and flanked by pots of foliage plants, becomes the best seat in the house for capturing the garden's ongoing drama on paper.

natural studies
Today's garden stars become future art. Just-picked dwarf sunflowers pose in a vase. A potting bench doubles as an outdoor painting table.

careful observation
The crinkled leaves and delicate blossoms of scented geraniums delight the nose with their crisp fragrances and entice the eye with their textures. These frost-tender plants must come inside for the winter everywhere except along the mild-winter West Coast.

color
decor

structures 294
furnishings 296
a garden house 298
a vine pole 300
a trellis trio 302
containers 304
accessories 306
a patriotic scheme 308

structures

the bigger picture

Garden structures play a major role as ambassadors of color. They carry your chosen palette throughout the landscape in ways that plants can't. A vividly painted arbor or trellis fills in the gaps at times when plant color has ebbed.

The first structure to consider? Your house. In fact, take a long look at your house's exterior before planting anything in the ground. You may hesitate to paint the entire house in your favorite hues, but consider shutters and the front door as the threshold of color possibilities.

open-and-shut color

right: Blue shutters or a blue garden bench alone might not have been sufficient to make this shady garden stand out. Repeating the color theme on both levels has more impact, especially when paired with pink blooms.

blue times two

left: In this narrow passage, the yellow gate stands in for flowers. Not visible is the garden beyond, liberally dotted with yellow blooms.

arizona zeal

below left: Outdoor fabric and painted concrete echo the intense blue of the desert sky.

shed chic

below right: The earthy tones of exterior stain turn an ordinary bench and shed into a magnetic setting.

furnishings

color feasts

Garden furniture gives you a vantage point for appreciating your finished garden painting. It also intensifies and completes the palette you begin with plants. A brilliant color, such as red or orange, becomes a full-fledged garden scheme when flowers have the companionship of a chair or a bench in the same hue.

Choices abound in garden styles of seating as well as materials and finishes. The style should take its cue from both house architecture and the feel of the garden. Among materials, choose cedar or teak for longevity and year-round outdoor endurance. If you plan to paint bare wood, then select cedar or pine. Plastic or resin chairs offer an economical, easy-to-wash alternative in garden furniture. Wicker looks natural, blends with most flower colors, and endows gardens with a classic casual look. For durability and a more formal fit, invest in metal furniture. Old metal or old wicker can be repainted with your favorite bright colors.

A seat flanked with colorfully planted pots creates focus in a small garden or a cozy corner in a large space. Place seating areas where they're shaded at least part of the day but with a full garden view. Add interest to a shady place with a chair or a bench painted in a luminous color.

take a seat

To tie a garden seat into background plantings, choose a similar color or complement. Old-fashioned Adirondack chairs offer timeless appeal with their casual comfort and easy-to-paint construction. *Clockwise from opposite top:* Green-painted ladderback chairs and a blue tablecloth contribute to a relaxing dining spot on an enclosed patio. A rosy pink makes surrounding flowers pop out of the shade. A bench cushion reflects the soft pastels of surrounding flowers. Blue-painted Adirondack chairs coordinate with gray flagstone and gravel, taking the color scheme a bolder step forward. A sunflower-color chair with a floral print cushion works with the plant scheme. A red chair makes the shade hum with color and looks crisp with the Shasta daisies.

a garden house

zones	make it	skill
all	1 month	advanced

you will need

- shovel
- concrete premix
- concrete blocks
- anchor bolts
- 2×4s, 1×6s
- salvaged windows
- salvaged door
- plexiglass
- clear vinyl tarp
- wood siding
- architectural details (optional)
- exterior-grade paint or stain

plant playhouse

Hatch your garden's color scheme in a cozy greenhouse that requires minimal woodworking skills. The fairytale charm of this building (*right*) derives from the doors and windows gathered from thrift shops and neighbors' throwaways.

Erect your garden house on a concrete foundation. Excavate, then use concrete blocks to frame the foundation. Fill and cover the blocks with concrete. While the concrete is wet, insert anchor bolts and leave half of each protruding above the concrete surface. Allow several days for the concrete to cure. Drying time depends on the weather.

Construct the house's framework in sections to accommodate the windows, door, walls, and roof. Use a plexiglass roof that withstands wind and hail better than glass but admits light just as well. Make the edges leakproof by fastening a clear vinyl tarp over the roof. Build benches along the interior walls of the shed to hold potted plants and seedling trays, if you like. Leave the dirt floor bare, or cover it with a few inches of pea gravel.

garden hideaway

right: **A focal point in a shady backyard, this 5×9-foot greenhouse wears shades of serene green and periwinkle blue.**

1 frame Build a series of four 2×4 frames to accommodate the windows and door in your greenhouse plan. Join the house frames together to form walls, fastening them to the anchor bolts protruding from the concrete foundation. Attach the roof rafters, made of 2×4s, to the tops of the walls. The roof shown is steeply pitched to fit a special stained-glass window at one end. You may want a flatter roof.

2 windows and doors Nail 1×6s horizontally across the roof rafters to steady the rafters in place and serve as nailers for the plexiglass covering. Nail 2×4s upright in the front and back walls to stabilize the roof. Install windows in the wall frames. Install a door in one wall. You may need to trim the door to fit the opening. Nail wood siding to the outside walls. Add architectural trim or other details, if you like. Finish the house, using exterior-grade paint or stain.

3 special features Include a stained-glass window or pieces of decorative tile as a personal touch in your garden house design. Fit custom-cut glass around the window or tiles. Other options include a birdhouse, an old clock, a thermometer, or other found art. A practical design could include a window or a vent that opens and closes to help regulate the temperature and humidity in the house.

a vine pole

you will need

- two 8-foot-long 2×4s
- one 4-foot-long 1×4
- exterior-grade wood glue
- one 3-foot-long 1×6
- two 4-foot ¾-inch-diameter dowels cut into 6-inch pieces
- one 3½-inch (approx.) wood finial with dowel bolt
- four 3-inch-long galvanized deck screws
- exterior stain or sealer; or primer and paint

going up!

This 6-foot-tall structure gives your color garden an aerial accent. Plant it to prop annual vines, such as black-eyed Susan, morning glory, or sweet pea, or a perennial clematis, hardy kiwi, or climbing rose.

Cut 12 square spacers (4×4-inch) from 1×4 treated lumber. Starting at the top, locating the first spacer flush with the top ends of the 2×4s, glue the spacers (3½ inches apart) between a pair of treated 2×4s. Use exterior-grade wood glue and bond the spacers to the 2×4s; clamp them until the glue dries.

morning glory

right and *below:* **Give your flower garden a colorful lift with a pegged pole that supports vines, such as morning glories. Top the pole with a small birdhouse or a weather vane instead of a finial.**

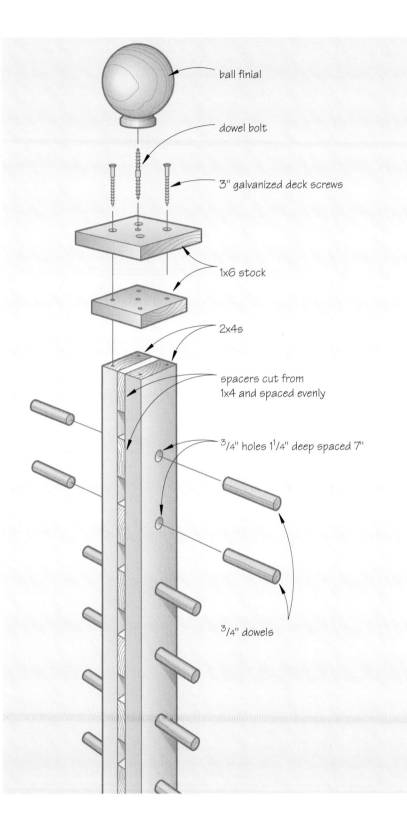

ball finial

dowel bolt

3" galvanized deck screws

1x6 stock

2x4s

spacers cut from
1x4 and spaced evenly

³/4" holes 1¹/4" deep spaced 7"

³/4" dowels

aim high

above: **Use cedar or pressure-treated lumber;
build two poles to create symmetrical shapes
at a garden entrance.**

Drill holes in the pole sides for the 6-inch
dowels and glue them in place. Cut the squares for
the top, as shown, from the 1×6 and screw them
into position using deck screws.

Fasten the ball finial to the top with a dowel
bolt (a specialty fastener that has screw threads
on both ends). Drill a pilot hole, and then twist the
bolt into the hole by gripping the center of it with
locking pliers.

Finish the wood with exterior stain or sealer;
or prime and paint it.

Set the pole in the ground at least 24 inches
deep to stabilize it.

a trellis trio

zones	make it	skill
all	1 day	moderate

you will need

- eight 8-foot-long 2×4s
- sixteen 8-foot-long 1×2s
- one 6-foot-long 2×10
- power miter saw
- 1¼-inch 3d galvanized nails
- deck screws
- exterior-grade wood glue
- 3-inch galvanized deck screws
- saber saw
- crushed rock
- exterior stain or sealer; or primer and paint

garden dividers

Every room should have a versatile piece of furniture that accomplishes many functions. This trellis trio performs the same feat in a garden room. Not only do they support vines, but when stood together, the structures form a corner screen. Placed side by side, this trellis trio creates a privacy fence beautifully cloaked in vines or climbing roses.

Begin building them by taking six of the eight 2×4 posts and cutting a 30-degree angle at the top end, using a power miter saw for best results. Cut the 1×2 brackets and center each side-to-side inside a post, with the top end 1½ inches from the angled cut on the post. Nail the brackets in place.

To make the lattice part of the trellis, first create points at the tops of the nine 1×2 uprights by cutting two 45-degree angles; then cut the uprights to the right length. Cut the 1×2 trellis rails, then nail those and the uprights together to form the lattice.

topping off a green scene

right: Vine pole, fence, and screen in one, this triad of trellises supports climbing plants and provides playful shapes to pique visual interest. When stood together, the structures can form a corner screen.

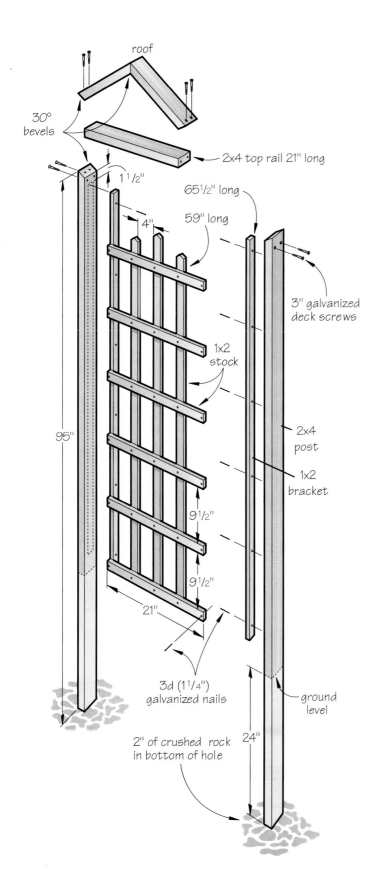

roof

30°
bevels

2x4 top rail 21" long

1 1/2"

65 1/2" long

59" long

4"

3" galvanized
deck screws

1x2
stock

95"

2x4
post

1x2
bracket

9 1/2"

9 1/2"

21"

3d (1 1/4")
galvanized nails

ground
level

2" of crushed rock
in bottom of hole

24"

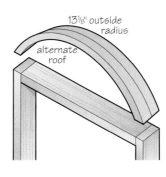

13 1/8" outside
radius

alternate
roof

Cut a 2×4 to make
the top rail 21 inches
long. Position the rail
between the tops of
the posts, and drive
deck screws into
countersunk pilot holes
to secure it. Nail the
lattice to the brackets.
Finish by cutting the
top pieces and screwing them into position.

Create the arched trellis top by cutting the post
tops square as shown *at left*. Glue the 2×10s face-
to-face. To draw the radius, use a piece of string
tied between a pencil and a brad. Cut the radius
using a saber saw.

Finish the trellises using exterior stain or sealer;
or prime and paint them.

To anchor each trellis in the ground, dig two
holes 26 inches deep for each post. Pour 2 inches
of crushed rock into the bottom of each hole to
provide drainage.

triple treasure
above: **Use cedar or pressure-treated lumber to
make your trellis trio.**

ultimate yard & garden | **303**

containers

carried away

Garden containers are like the pumpkin in the Cinderella story that becomes an extraordinary vehicle. With a little paint or polish, any ordinary vessel gleaned from a garage sale, thrift shop, or junk pile could turn into magical transportation for your plants.

Transform pots, planters, boxes, baskets, wheelbarrows, wagons, or any containers that offer colorful charm into homes for plants. Situate a spectacular urn or other shapely vessel where it makes an outstanding contribution to the garden on its own. Use containers to decorate an entrance or brighten a corner. Choose vessels of weather-resistant materials that coordinate with the style of your house or garden.

ageless style

above right: **A vintage watering can adds an elegant touch to a traditional garden.**

paint buckets

right: **Display color on a picket fence by painting galvanized French flower buckets with two coats of enamel paint. Drill a hole in the bottom of each bucket for drainage, and plant, or don't drill but fill with fresh cut flowers. Hang buckets on cup hooks.**

rub-a-dub tub

above: A galvanized tub with awning stripes transforms a garden corner. Paint contrasting stripes in minutes or rub on a metallic finish to give the tub an aged look. Fill the container with ice and bottled drinks for a garden party.

magical mystery

left: A tall ceramic urn glows among the grasses. Its color is related to the encircling tapestry of greens but with just enough blue to stand out. The urn provides color and an architectural counterpoint to flowing grasses and shrubbery. Whether planted or chosen to make an artful statement on its own, a large, beautifully glazed container works magic in any garden.

accessories

fun with color

Garden ornaments add the finishing touches to your garden. Take advantage of the opportunity to express your personality as you integrate decorative elements with a focus on color.

Find garden ornaments among the everyday things stashed in your basement or garage, in salvage shops, or at yard sales. If the object of your desire is chipped, cracked, or faded, so much the better for its future life outdoors. A fresh coat of paint to highlight your garden's colors gives it a new life.

sunny side

right: Work bird habitats into your color scheme. A bright yellow birdhouse glows in early-morning light. Birds won't appreciate the paint job, but you will.

step-by-step art

left: Mosaic stepping-stones turn broken dishes into garden art. They're easily assembled with wet concrete and a round or square mold. Embed the mosaic design while the concrete is still wet.

pretty in pink

below: Plastic flamingos peek out of a patch of feathery ferns, enlivening the garden with their classic appeal. Gather a flock for the most impact and a little humor.

a patriotic scheme

zones	make it	skill
all	weekend	easy

you will need

one 8–foot–long 2×2

exterior paint (red, white, blue, gold)

drill

exterior-grade wood glue

five flags on dowels/sticks

5–inch–diameter wooden ball (optional)

jigsaw

four 3–inch–diameter wooden stars

five 2–inch–long–, ¼–inch–diameter dowels

shovel

concrete pre–mix (optional)

ten 2–foot–long, ¼–inch–diameter dowels

string

red petunias, white vinca, and blue salvia

old glory garden

Based on an old custom of raising the liberty pole every Fourth of July, this flag pole garden waves the red, white, and blue at its top and bottom.

The patriotic planting of annuals echoes the flag colors in a star-shape bed. A blooming replica of the flag is more complicated but doable in a large area.

When planting, amass plants in groups of each color for best results. Use red, white, and blue petunias only, or choose alternative plants, such as verbena, pansy, ageratum (blue and white varieties); and red salvia, verbena, or dwarf snapdragon.

Pluck and trim faded blossoms to keep the garden's color waving through the summer. Fertilize once a month.

For how-to instructions about garden projects go to **www.bhg.com/bkgardenprojects**

flowering tribute

right: Red petunias, blue salvia, and white vinca echo the patriotic theme in a star-shape garden.

1 assemble pole Make the (8-sided) pole by beveling the four edges of a 2×2. Paint the pole red, white, and blue. Six inches below the pole's top, drill four holes at angles to hold the flags. Embellish the pole with a gold ball at the top and white stars below, if desired. Paint the ball gold; let it dry. Drill ¼-inch holes in the ball's top and bottom and the pole's top. Glue and insert a 2-inch-long dowel into the ball's bottom; mount it in the pole's top. Insert a flag in the ball's top.

2 embellish Cut four 3-inch stars from wood, or buy precut stars from a crafts store and paint them white. Drill a ¼-inch hole in the side of each star. Glue and insert the end of the 2-inch dowels into each star. Repeat this process to attach each dowel to the pole. Dig a 2-foot-deep hole and set the flag pole in place. Refill the hole and firmly tamp the soil. Or anchor the pole in concrete, if you like.

3 stellar planting Arrange five stakes in a circle around the pole at points equidistant from the pole and one another. Place five more stakes in a smaller circle, at points in between the first circle of stakes, equidistant from the pole and one another. Use string to outline a star. Tie the string to an outer-circle stake, run it to an inner-circle stake, wrap it around the stake, run it to an outer-circle stake, and so on from stake to stake. Remove sod inside the outline; amend the soil. Plant annuals in a red, white, and blue pattern.

resources

mail–order nurseries, garden suppliers, artists/gardeners, and others

American Horticulture Society (AHS) (B)
7931 East Boulevard Dr.
Alexandria, VA 22308
703/768-5700
www.ahs.org

Burpee Co. (S, H)
300 Park Ave.
Warminster, PA 18974
800/333-5808
www.burpee.com

Forestfarm (P)
990 Tetherow Rd.
Williams, OR 97544-9599
541/846-7269
www.forestfarm.com

Gardener's Supply Co. (H)
128 Intervale Rd.
Burlington, VT 05401
888/833-1412
www.gardeners.com

Greer Gardens (P)
1280 Goodpasture Island Rd.
Eugene, OR 97401
541/686-8266
www.greergardens.com

Heirloom Roses (P)
24062 NE Riverside Dr.
St. Paul, OR 97137
503/538-1576
www.heirloomroses.com

Heronswood Nursery (P)
7530 NE 288th St.
Kingston, WA 98346
360/297-4172
www.heronswood.com

High Country Gardens (P, H)
2902 Rufina St.
Santa Fe, NM 87507-2929
800/925-9387
www.highcountrygardens.com

Hortico Nurseries Inc. (P)
723 Robson Rd., RR #1
Waterdown, Ontario LOR 2H1
Canada
905/689-6984
www.hortico.com

Hydrangeas Plus (P)
P.O. Box 389
Aurora, OR 97002
866/433-7896
www.hydrangeasplus.com

Jackson & Perkins (P, H)
1 Rose Ln.
Medford, OR 97501
877/322-2300
www.jacksonandperkins.com

Kinsman Co. (H)
P.O. Box 428
Pipersville, PA 18947
800/733-4146
www.kinsmangarden.com

Maryjo Koch
555 Martin Rd.
Santa Cruz, CA 95060
831/425-7422
www.maryjokoch.com

Valerie Murray
Abkhazi Garden
1964 Fairfield Rd.
Victoria, BC Canada
250/598-8096

Musser Forests (H, P)
1880 Route 119, Hwy N
Indiana, PA 15701
800/643-8319
www.musserforests.com

Netherlands Flower Bulb
Information Center (B)
www.bulb.com

Niche Gardens (P)
1111 Dawson Rd.
Chapel Hill, NC 27516
919/967-0078
www.nichegdn.com

Perennial Plant Association (PPA) (B)
3383 Schirtzinger Rd.
Hilliard, OH 43026
614/771-8431
www.perennialplant.org

Plant Delights Nursery (P)
9241 Sauls Rd.
Raleigh, NC 27603
919/772-4794
www.plantdelights.com

Proven Winners (P)
111 E. Elm Street, Suite D
Sycamore, IL 60178
877/865-5818
www.provenwinners.com

Roslyn Nursery (B)
211 Burrs Ln.
Dix Hills, NY 11746
631/643-9347
www.roslynnursery.com

Safari Thatch and Bamboo (H)
2056 N. Dixie Hwy.
Fort Lauderdale, FL 33305
954/564-7021
www.safarithatch.com

John Scheepers, Inc. (P)
23 Tulip Dr.
Bantam, CT 06750
860/567-0838
www.johnscheepers.com

Sherwin-Williams Co. (H)
www.sherwin-williams.com

Smith & Hawken (H)
P.O. Box 8690
Pueblo, CO 81008-9998
800/940-1170
www.smithandhawken.com

Karen Strohbeen (B)
The Perennial Gardener's Journal
www.pbs.org/perennialgardener

Chris Keylock Williams (B)
6213 SE Main St.
Portland, OR 97215
503/233-7314
www.chriskeylockwilliams.com

Thompson & Morgan, Inc. (S)
220 Faraday Ave.
Jackson, NJ 08527
800/274-7333
www.thompson-morgan.com

Tranquil Lake Nursery (P)
45 River St.
Rehoboth, MA 02769-1395
508/252-4002
www.tranquil-lake.com

Van Bourgondien (P)
P.O. Box 2000
Virginia Beach, VA 23450-2000
800/622-9959
www.dutchbulbs.com

Wayside Gardens (P)
1 Garden Ln.
Hodges, SC 29695-0001
800/213-0379
www.waysidegardens.com

White Flower Farm (P)
P.O. Box 50, Route 63
Litchfield, CT 06759
800/503-9624
www.whiteflowerfarm.com

Woodlanders (P)
1128 Colleton Ave.
Aiken, SC 29801
803/648-7522
www.woodlanders.net

usda plant hardiness zone maps

These maps of climate zones can help you select plants for your garden that will survive a typical winter in your region. The United States Department of Agriculture (USDA) developed the map for North America, basing the zones on the lowest recorded temperatures. On a scale of 1 to 11, Zone 1 is the coldest area and Zone 11 is the warmest.

Plants are classified in zones by the coldest temperature they can endure. For example, plants hardy to Zone 6 survive where winter temperatures drop to –10° F. Those hardy to Zone 8 would die long before it's that cold. These plants may grow in colder regions but must be replaced each year. Plants rated for a range of hardiness zones can usually survive winter in the coldest region, as well as tolerate the summer heat of the warmest one.

To find your hardiness zone, note the approximate location of your community on the map; then match the color marking that area to the key.

Make sure your plants will flourish in the weather in your area. Consult the last spring frost map, the first autumn frost map, and detailed state-specific hardiness maps at **www.bhg.com/bkzonemaps**

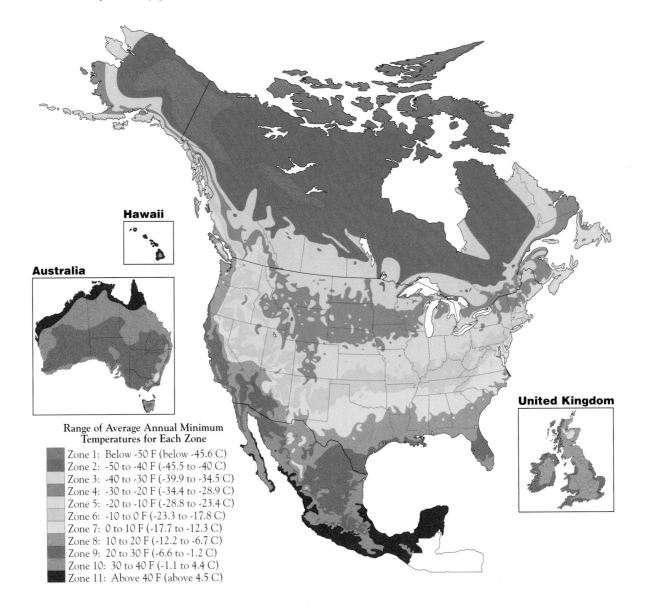

Hawaii

Australia

United Kingdom

Range of Average Annual Minimum Temperatures for Each Zone

Zone 1: Below -50 F (below -45.6 C)
Zone 2: -50 to -40 F (-45.5 to -40 C)
Zone 3: -40 to -30 F (-39.9 to -34.5 C)
Zone 4: -30 to -20 F (-34.4 to -28.9 C)
Zone 5: -20 to -10 F (-28.8 to -23.4 C)
Zone 6: -10 to 0 F (-23.3 to -17.8 C)
Zone 7: 0 to 10 F (-17.7 to -12.3 C)
Zone 8: 10 to 20 F (-12.2 to -6.7 C)
Zone 9: 20 to 30 F (-6.6 to -1.2 C)
Zone 10: 30 to 40 F (-1.1 to 4.4 C)
Zone 11: Above 40 F (above 4.5 C)